John Watterson, as a research chemist in the U.S. Geological Survey 1966–1995, published many papers and edited various books on prospecting using the surface geochemical and biogeochemical signatures of subsurface mineral deposits.

John's research on the possible use of a common spore-forming soil bacterium in mineral exploration resulted in wide commercial and academic interest and in many invitations to speak. He calls it a fun career.

In retirement, John has been active in a small-town writing group in western Colorado. His poems are of the widest scope, candid and evocative. They can invite the reader under a coverslip, into a gopher hole, or into the infinite region enclosing our universe.

Mostly to Bill and Bob who came rowing along in their invisible rowboat just when I needed them.

John Watterson

POEMS ON ETERNITY, THE ENDLESS UNIVERSE, AND ME

AUSTIN MACAULEY PUBLISHERS™

LONDON • CAMBRIDGE • NEW YORK • SHARJAH

Ordering Information
Quantity sales: Special discounts are available on quantity purchases by corporations, associations, and others. For details, contact the publisher at the address below.

Publisher's Cataloging-in-Publication data
Watterson, John
Poems on Eternity, the Endless Universe, and Me

ISBN 9781685622237 (Paperback)
ISBN 9781685622244 (Hardback)
ISBN 9781685622268 (ePub e-book)
ISBN 9781685622251 (Audiobook)

Library of Congress Control Number: 2023903323

www.austinmacauley.com/us

First Published 2023
Austin Macauley Publishers LLC
40 Wall Street, 33rd Floor, Suite 3302
New York, NY 10005
USA

mail-usa@austinmacauley.com
+1 (646) 5125767

Ten Minutes in the Grocery Line

I assume with recent cosmologists
that the life of our universe,
including the larger black holes,
is about 10^{100} years.
Since it is possible conceptually
to compress 10^{100} years into
one thousandth of a second,
some 600,000 universes like ours
could burst into flower and evaporate
one after another
in the ten minutes it takes
to reach the checkout counter.
The checkout lady smiles at me.
She knows I've been waiting a long time.

The Zeppelin Hangar

When I was eight my dad took me to see an empty dirigible hangar,
the biggest empty building I'd ever seen.
We were the only two there. There was just enough light to see
the immensity of it.
My father's stunning imagination in doing this
has turned it into a zeppelin hangar, even bigger;
and I am now alone in it, so to speak.
This zeppelin hangar is my unconscious mind,
the *Unbewust* – the unknown that Jung called God,
something not entirely unknown to me
since nothing would be there if it had not passed through consciousness,
consciousness being what is lit up by the beam of my small flashlight.
It is the Forgotten part of me that directs everything.
The beautiful sparrow I shot with my BB gun is there,
and it keeps me from harming sparrows.

My father is all through that hangar like invisible webbing.
He is flying air-sea rescue in a PBY,
bringing back shot-down fighter pilots
in the Battle of Leyte Gulf.
He fills the zeppelin hangar.

As a kid my dad never had a .410 shotgun,
a Silver King bicycle or a Whizzer.
He had three brothers and two sisters—it was the Depression.
His preacher dad was too poor,
too stern and unworldly to relish his sons.
But my dad bought these things for me,

picked them out himself at Hawley Hardware
and Western Auto.
He never had a tree house,
but climbed up and admired mine.
He never had a motorcycle, but he helped me fix mine,
in fact took me to the motorcycle races in Dodge City
in 1952 when I was fourteen.
Admired the Ariel Square Fours with me,
their fighter-plane-like sound.

Fourteen in 1931, he worked on 'Gramp McBurney's' farm,
then with his older brother John rode the rails
to Idaho to pick potatoes. His fun had to be
breaking loose from a hell-fire-and-damnation father,
playing his harmonica on top of a moving boxcar,
smoking and laughing with the hobos,
in collecting a promise from a frisky farm girl…

Then delivering milk in the middle of the night,
working his way through medical school,
selling his blood more often than you're supposed to.
His fun was being a flight surgeon on that aircraft carrier,
His fun had to be in being an authentic healer,
and then maybe, in looking through my eyes
at the at the big crowd at his funeral,
and in finally understanding his greatness,

Discovering Tao Yuan-Ming

If I am ever greeted by an angel
I know who she will be.
I had had a few drinks in Mozambique
with the crew of the Stella Lykis.
Somehow I ended up alone.
True, it was a cheap little place.
Full of people, noise and music.
Then it was silent.
Hadijah was standing there
three feet away,
I could tell she was a prophetess.
I saw a child light in her eyes
that was surely illegal.
The hang of her skirt bereft me of reason,
might have converted St. Paul.
Her smile was an unplanned lobotomy.
She had to take charge of me,
leading me away in a trance.
In bed she told me her name.
Though she was black as black could be
I remember briefly thinking
"Is there any chance
she would marry me?"
If I could have better remembered that night
it might have saved me years of drinking.
In the morning when the sun was up
I put a lot of money on her bed,
weeping helplessly.

Hadijah smiled and shrugged,
making it a votive offering.
That morning in a bookstore
I discovered Tao Yuan-Ming.

Trying to Imagine Infinity

If our galaxy were the size of a penny here in Delta
the observational horizon of our universe would be 20 miles away
somewhere around Hotchkiss.
Because of inflation, however, the true "edge" is actually much further,
even thousands or millions of miles beyond Hotchkiss.
Or let's be modest, even medieval.
If the edge is only, say, 200 miles away at this scale,
then the universe we see is only a millionth part of what is there,
hardly a representative sample!
If the edge is 2,000 miles away, a not unreasonable proposal,
then what we see is only a billionth part of the actual volume
of what we call "our" universe.
What is more, it now seems reasonable to many cosmologists
that an uncountable number of other universes exist,
the majority of which do not contain observers.
Fortunately, the imagination is not limited by the speed of light,
by actual distances or strict accountability.
I am buried deep within a galaxy of one hundred billion stars,
the galaxy itself being one among a hundred billion we can see…
in a universe the size of which we cannot guess,
so much larger is it than our telescopes suggest.
Just one of an unimaginable number of universes.
Still I imagine I can imagine it.
What haunts me is the idea
that the whole thing can somehow be imagined.
I believe this is the trick:
At the scale in which infinity is meaningful

the unimaginably monstrous universes in it
are infinitely small,
have lost any perceptible dimension;
they are, let us say, present only in thought.
Light, at this scale, will have stopped and cannot inform us.
Absolute Nothingness prevails.

Giordano Bruno

In the year 1600 Giordano Bruno was burned at the stake
by the inerrant Vatican for refusing to give up the idea of infinity.
I too am sometimes obtuse enough
to indulge in similar imagining.
It is a scale problem involving time and space.
I like to think it reasonable to imagine a dark, cold space
where I *only know* that tiny universes and clusters of universes
are being formed, expanding and evaporating
through proton decay and lasting only for the blink of an eye,
say 10^{100} years.
At such a scale infinity is more meaningful (if still infinity).
Nothing whatever is to be seen.
The most violent supernovae cast no light
from a universe to an outside observer
because, at an expanding universe's periphery,
light will have died, flat-lined out.
So from outside, universes will be dark,
no tell-tale radiation anywhere.
This is the ultimate vision I come up with.
We are where only the imagination works.
There is no choice but to assume this place goes on forever.
But how to investigate it if there is nothing to see
(or even imagine) and there is nothing whatever to orient one?
The question, naturally, regards the extent of infinity. Ha!
The great secret, I suspect, is that we needn't travel to find out.
We are already there.
In measureless, eternal Nothing,
the God of the Sufi mystics.

Joking Eyes

She only came twice to our meeting;
no one else paid attention to her.
Both times she sat next to me,
once on my left, once on my right.
Did I send out radiation?
She seemed completely at home.
I'm not sure I knew what it was 'til then
to see music in a woman's eyes.
A Vivaldi concerto?
There was something modestly happy
when she smiled and politely glanced at me
the two or three times she spoke;
I heard not a word she said.
I only saw the vivacity,
the quick movement of her eyes,
the easy change from solemnity
to darting apogee,
a secret jokingness that showed
knowledge of all the world's secrets.

And if in fact she was possessed
of comprehensive knowledge,
she will have known, or at least guessed,
the conclusion of Rabbi Dov Baer,
that he could see in such eyes,
eyes willing to share
their heavenly laughter, magic itself,
his own dear God advertising Himself.

My Love Affair with Anna

I met Anna in a Saturday afternoon Bible class.
She had a small backpack and canvas gym shoes,
the kind that come up to your ankles.
She was 75 at the time, I was 38.
I got to taking her home after class.
She had escaped the Nazis the year I was born.
I did have to take her to a 'tea' my wife arranged,
to make sure things were on the up and up.
After that there was no problem at home about Anna.
Aristotle was right about the problematical nature
of friendship between men and women;
but when it came to Anna he was wrong.
I loved her dearly, enough to take her to
pro bono dentist appointments and whatnot
that hardly seemed recompense for her friendship.
She was fluent in Hungarian, German,
English, Spanish, French and Italian; she could read and write
Greek, Latin and Hebrew. After a few weeks of marriage as a
girl in Budapest she decided marriage was not for her.
She followed her '*luftmensch*' father
and became a scholar instead.
I would sometimes spend an hour with her during the week.
We would speculate on incompletely resolved questions:
like what Maimonides really thought about Moses,
what Strauss really thought about Maimonides,
or what Scholem really thought about Strauss.
I wondered whether there were Sabbatians,
maybe Budapest Frankists among her forebears,

but I didn't ask. We talked about all sorts of things
you can't talk about with other people.

I used to kiss her when I let her out of the car.
One time she said I was the light of her life.
She lived to be 99. I know I'll never find another like her.

"The Place"

As I read him, Hasdai Crescas,
who died in 1410 or 1412,
a philosopher, statesman and mystic—
had quite the same idea of an infinite
multiverse as do modern cosmologists.
He grappled with the idea of an infinite
universe-containing abyss, a vacuum.
Giordano Bruno seems to have borrowed
some of his arguments.
What most interests me about Crescas
was his concept of God.
"The Place" (*ha-Makom*), a Talmudic appellation of God, strikes Crescas
as a remarkable metaphor.
I think I understand why.
When I consider "The Place"
as Crescas considered it—a region of unimaginable vastness—
I tend to think of it
in the most parochial ant-like way, that is,
from a region in this vastness
where there are universes;
but that only confuses me.
It is far better to think
of the vast emptiness itself,
where universes
and clusters of universes

are unnoticeable
transitory disruptions.
My best understanding of "The Place"
thus includes everything,
uninterrupted silence, darkness, harmony.

Loneliness

Eckhart, Buber and others
spoke of what happens there
in special solitary moments
as incommunicable,
an *istigheit*, an *is*ness
for which words
have not been fashioned.
A major consequence of this
would appear to be
an irredeemable loneliness,
the circumstance that every living thing
every grubworm,
is in solitary confinement
from which words cannot escape.
This itself amounts
to something that cannot be said.
But an even more significant consequence,
is that I share this imprisonment;
I am the same
as every sparrow,
stray cat,
homeless man.
Our loneliness is a continuous thread,
no matter our distractions;
we have a perfect
wireless connection.
We don't even have to look at each other.
We *are* each other.

A Certain Woman

A certain ineffable woman is anorexic.
The brightness of her eyes,
the impossible brightness
of her smile,
the absence of restraint
in her smiling kiss and hug
devastate me, turn me inside out.
For a while I intentionally avoided
meetings she goes to,
so that after a few months
I might not think of her so much.
When we meet again
I have difficulty recognizing her,
and it makes my heart stop.
Even though she is another man's wife
I do not count it apostasy
to kiss her cheek
and whisper that I love her.
I keep the pain to myself.
If I could act out my desire
I would ask her
to let me hold her for an hour;

but since that would be so like a drink,
holding her must remain a fantasy.
Rather, I must leave it to some more intrepid
microflake of ash that remains of me
to seek out a particle of hers.
Then something stronger than the strong force
would take over, we would survive dissolution,
and she would smile at me forever.
Her hologram smile would be part of me forever.

A Drop of Water

If I should be
no more than a drop of water,
I would reflect on Avogadro's number*
and remind myself of the six thousand billion billion
redoubtable molecules I contain,
all of which, having been repeatedly split
and recombined,
are as fresh as they were when scattered
in supernovae several billion years ago.
My lusty molecules
have lurked for millions of years
in subducting sediments,
popped out in volcanic steam,
ready to do it over again.
I danced when photosynthesis invented itself
never fretting the loss of covalent bonds.
Was I nervous when a stegosaurus was frightened?
Who was I to mind being peed away
when I was later to reflect the face of Narcissus.
I may now be the least remarkable part of a quiet pond
but some of my number
were just a little while ago creating a happy waterfall,
whizzing off to become a cloud.
Several of me watched torpedoes speeding by
on the way to the Arizona,
fell as rain on the grave of Leonidas.
Of the warhorse in Job
I was in the sweat,

in the glory of his nostrils,
in the thunder of his neck.
I am just a muddy drop,
but what I have been!
What I will be!

*One mole—a gram-molecular weight—of water (18 grams) will contain 6.02×10^{23} molecules. One raindrop, 0.18 g, will contain 6×10^{21} or six thousand billion billion molecules. Some idea of the dense construction of this one drop can be had by imagining a pipe a quarter mile in diameter reaching to the moon. 6×10^{21} steel BBs would fill this pipe.

Leonidas

The very sight of Spartans exercising
and combing their hair
in front of the wall at Thermopylae
held up the incredulous Xerxes for five days,
waiting for them to flee his 300,000-man army*.
(Herodotus elsewhere makes it a million.)
After two days of fighting,
who knows how many Persians were lost.
Killing them was sport for the Greek hoplites.
But defeat at Thermopylae, always forgone,
occurred when the way over the mountain
was betrayed by the black-hearted Ephialtes,
may memory of him be lost.
Leonidas and his 300 picked Spartans
fought a rear-guard action, allowing
the otherwise doomed Greek army to escape.
Herodotus reports "a great struggle [occurred]
between the Persians and Lacedaemonians
over Leonidas' body till valorous Greeks
dragged it away and four times
put their enemies to flight."
All told, they held up the Persians for a week,
long enough to humiliate and infuriate Xerxes
who ordered Leonidas' corpse mutilated,
his head placed on a pike.
Herodotus was perhaps weeping
when he wrote the lines about the stone lion
that now stands at the mouth of the pass

in honor of Leonidas and his men.
God himself must weep
to think he could have made such men.

*This estimate (300,000) is from a contemporary verse cited by Herodotus (Great Books VII 228). The Greek force Leonidas and his 300 men saved consisted of six thousand volunteers who had joined them. Herodotus twice mentions (208f.) that before battle some of the Spartans could be seen at exercise in front of the wall with others combing their [long] hair. It was a pan-Mediterranean practice at this time to let one's hair grow in preparation for war. For a few Spartans to sit combing their hair before the Persian host was so incredible a taunt as to cause Xerxes to marvel

Solipsism

My atrial flutter,
when it occurs,
makes me a solipsist,
instantly displaces
my delusion
of a substantial self,
makes me realize
that all I see
and imagine,
the tender horizon,
the *ur*abyss beyond,
the Great Nothing,
starts and stops with me.
This must be
what it means
that when nothing occurs
I achieve nothing,
lack nothing,
experience nothing.
Why is it
that this weakness I have
should so amplify, almost explode
the tenderness I have
toward my friend,
my timid friend?

Mabel's Quick Massage Parlor *or*
Our Friday Morning Call

Hi Honey.
How're things in Albuquerque?
How's the knee?
You and Shannon getting some boxes packed?
Good deal.
The cats are fine.
Bob's asleep in my chair.
Mattie's had her medicine. No hairballs so far.
I watered your plants.
Litterboxes, everything's fine.

Me today? Actually I thought
I might treat myself
to a quick massage…uhm…at Mabel's Quick Massage Parlor.

No, Mabel doesn't make appointments.
She said to just come on by,
she'd have an opening for me.

But Honey, I've got some serious stiffness
in my back…
Mabel said she could loosen me up,
unkink my libido or something…

Yes, you're right, Honey, I'm just kidding.
Half an hour in the sauna

will fix it.
I miss you too, Honey.
Talk to you later. Bye.

Sam Johnson on Poetry

Samuel Johnson, that bear of a man,
did not answer immediately,
but after ten seconds or so, declaimed
that rhyme was better
than blank verse…in fact
the 'real thing' of poetry itself.
His opinion, even more
than how he felt about us colonials,
always disturbs me.
For my part
it's something about
the way I breathe
that makes rhyming store-bought.
I stultify, pollute myself,
if I get to thinking
things must rhyme.
It's such a vexatious
waste of time
if I get to thinking
things must rhyme.

Joseph K

Both times I've found myself traduced
I've studied Joseph K.
I marvel at the flippant way
he maintains his delusions.

The thing that always puzzles me
is the absence of a dignity
he surely must have had.

It seems to me piquant the way
that casual sex throughout the day
could seem so natural
to this distracted man.

It's no less strange to picture him
holding hands with Uncle Jim
while walking down the boulevard.
Was this also casual sex?

The ending couldn't be more dark—the grave he goes to in the park—
and lets the rabbis stab him.

A Glimpse of the Earth

There was a time when I scaled the earth
and the solar system for fun,
always a theoretical exercise.
One day on the wall of my office at the Survey
I drew an arc with a radius of five feet
to represent half of the earth.
Doing the math I saw
that the width of my thumbnail
at the top of the arc
would be forty miles.
A few weeks later,
assistant to a taciturn geologist,
driving south in the Basin and Range
of southwestern Nevada,
I realized that the horizon ahead was often
about forty miles away.
Visualizing my thumb
on my office wall,
in relation to what I saw,
I was able for a moment to grasp
the massiveness of the turning earth.
I had never guessed it was so big.
Nor have I ever been able to convey
the amazement I felt.
I thought: "I live here."

Rutabagas

The neighbor lady
is friendly enough over the fence,
good-looking
and, well, built.
When I see her hoeing
between her rutabagas,
I can't help but wonder
if I shouldn't offer
to help her with her weeds.
I have my own hoe.

A Circle with Infinite Radii

Let us imagine the edge
of a circle with an infinite radius.
If the radius is truly infinite
few would disagree
that the circumference would be
for any inspected length
a perfectly, absolutely straight line.
Yet we remember that this is part of a circle
whose center lies an infinite distance away.
Suppose we imagine two radii
intersecting this straight-line circumference
at two points some enormous distance apart.
It is useful to reflect that wherever a radius line
intersects a circle's circumference
the radius line makes a 90-degree angle
with a tangent to the circle at that point.
This has an interesting consequence:
all infinite radii on our side of the circle
(the only side we can consider)
are parallel.
By the definition of a "circle"
these two radii must meet
at the circle's center
some infinite distance away.
Aristotle, with his notion
of a finite infinity,
would say, I think,
that to satisfy definition

there <u>must</u> be in these two radii
an infinitesimally small deviation from parallelity,
one too small to be measured.
But this is a copout, like Crescas said,
and makes infinity finite.
Could there be this small deviation?
No.
If we are to take infinity seriously,
the radii, no matter how far apart,
on our straight-line arc
would be absolutely parallel.
The infinite center
would be where these parallel lines meet:
never!
If one believes in straight lines,
an infinite circle
is impossible.
Aristotle must have been nodding off
in Plato's lecture.

a'Kempis' Advice

Nowhere is the credo of a misanthrope
better put
than in a'Kempis admonition
to delight above all things
in being unknown and unregarded.
Even trees defy this,
straining every fiber
to be glorious,
putting on
impossibly immodest blossoms.
Maybe bottom-feeding carp
observe a'Kempis rule
now and then.
But even they
sometimes gain carp notoriety,
muscling others out of the way
to get a dead crawfish.
I like Lucretius' observation
that if one has become
an object of scorn
in the senate,
a few days of staying home
takes care of it.
The senate will have found
a new victim.
I myself go in and out
with this rule.
What I mostly notice

is, for example,
that when I really focus
on Wolfson's explanation
of Crescas' arguments
I experience the relish
a'Kempis refers to:
reading Crescas trumps
whatever party I am missing.
I have a need to go out
pretty regularly, quite regularly.
If I can remain aware
and restrain my impulse to talk,
I can return home
without thinking myself
a lesser man.
But come what may,
I can find myself
in the frame of mind
of Kafka
when he asked Brod
to burn his manuscripts;
or of Jules Verne
when he actually burned his.
Meanwhile, I know
that understanding
what I have understood
remains unperturbed,
inviolate.
In this I am perdurably aligned
with a'Kempis.

My Father

Because of their Samurai nature
certain men,
like mystics and feral tomcats,
don't live long,
burn themselves out,
use themselves up:
Alexander, Caesar, Napoleon,
immortals like Audie Murphy.
I am only now realizing it,
but my dad was like that.
It made my life easy and long
—the most I ever had was turmoil,
like that poor man
Randolph Churchill.
On my deathbed
I will weep for my father.

Feeling Sorry for Myself

When I was forty years old
Maimonides was my guide.
I tried to live according to something he said
in the *Eight Chapters*:
"Never try to be funny."
At seventy-four I sometimes try to be funny,
though every time I do
I make a bow to Maimonides.
'Be serious at all costs'
could have been my slogan.
Now if someone is like that they're stuffy.
At seventy-four I feel
that my life is about over,
despite the fact that
I have friends much older.
I just ask myself:
what am I waiting around for?
There are some happy things—
at the picnic accompanying Riley on the spoons,
riding my motorcycle in a storm,
thinking I might comfort a dying friend.
I guess the problem is
that whatever zest for accomplishment I've had
has gone south.
I keep thinking: I'm capable of infatuation

with someone or something,
but it doesn't happen,
and I see through it anyway.
Is this what is known as
becoming stolid?

More on Hasdai Crescas

The first of the Ten Commandments
begins: I am the Lord thy God...
(that brought thee out of the Land of Egypt,
out of the house of bondage.)
Unlike the rest of the apodictic,
unanswerable commandments,
the first commandment—if it is a commandment—
requires only belief
in God's existence and authority,
belief in the statement itself.
Maimonides formalized this belief,
made it not only a commandment
but a defining principle of Judaism.

An intrepid and lucid Spanish rabbi,
Hasdai Crescas, fully six centuries ago,
took both Moses and Maimonides
(if not the whole Jewish people)
to task, evidently on the basis
of his own experience if you can believe that.
He wrote
that a man is not responsible for his beliefs,
for belief is independent of the will.
(Freud would agree.)
Hence the First Commandment
is not a commandment,
but a preface.

Hasdai also took Aristotle to task
(much as a modern physicist might do)
for his disbelief in vacuum
and for hedging on infinity.
Talk about chutzpah! To justly correct
Moses, Aristotle, and Maimonides! Whoa!
What a wonderful thing it is
that certain men have lived.

Sharon

This is my friend Sharon.
She is one serious woman,
She can sometimes be
emphatic, incontrovertible.
Sponsors the whole world.
She used to scare me.
What changed all that
was when she
came back from Akron
and shed tears telling about
going through Dr. Bob's house.
All of a sudden she was
a great favorite of mine,
and has been ever since.

———

I never knew exactly what
Sharon's emotion was
at Dr. Bob's house
until I heard that
on Bill's grave
there is always
a small pile
of chips.

A Useful Aphorism

Unlike Socrates at 73,
I find I still take
an interest in certain women
that's not entirely intellectual.
I keep forgetting
the useful saying of a friend,
that when you're old
chasing women
is like elk hunting.
Sometimes it's better
not to get one.

The Intelligent Universe

There are at least a hundred billion stars in our galaxy.
It is arguable that one star in every thousand has a planet like ours
capable of supporting life, a minimum guess.
It is arguable that at least one in every thousand
life-supporting planets will in the course of their history
evolve a higher civilization.
If even one percent of these special planets is flourishing now,
it means we currently have
a thousand intelligent neighbors in our galaxy.
If this is true of our galaxy,
it will be true of all one hundred billion galaxies
in our visible universe.
In just the part of the universe we can see,
it means there are one hundred *trillion* planets
with civilizations something like ours.
The saying, "We are not alone,"
is thus grossly euphemistic.
So when I look at the night sky
it is humming with intelligence.
Over the integrated sum of billions of years
innumerable eyes are looking back at me.*

*Actually we are not so much looking at each other as imagining. We all have
the same library of stars, the oldest editions of which shined our way 13.7
billion years ago and whose copyrights have expired. Because of the dilatory
speed of light and where we are when we observe what appears to be a brand-
new star, it may have ceased to exist a billion or more years ago, before the
algae had evolved on our warm shores. In the same way, light streaming from

our star during our lifetime may not reach any of our intelligent contemporaries. We can only know that it will be a long time before light from the epoch we so prize will arrive at their telescopes. Isn't it interesting that for a hundred trillion or more cosmologist-bearing planets, neither Aristotle nor Jesus will yet have been born? So Michelson, in determining the speed of light, produced an algorithm for finding when the Advent will occur for a hundred trillion intelligent, unconverted planets. The Nobel committee seems to have overlooked this contribution.

The Meaning of a New Idea

The old idea was
that there was one universe,
and we were in it.
Aristotle, Newton and Einstein
thought there was nothing else.
The second idea
yet clung to by cosmologists
is corollary to the first—
that time began with the Big Bang.
The new idea of multiple universes,
is catastrophic
for both of these comforting notions.
If multiple universes exist,
they create the logical necessity
of a containing envelope, a vacuum abyss
in which these universes occur.
Since boundaries on the abyss
are inconceivable, the abyss has to be infinite.
Thus for the first time, infinity,
that mind-breaker, must be taken seriously.
So much for the first idea.
As to the idea of time,
the probability of multiple universes
renders obsolete the notion that time began
with the Big Bang that created *our* universe.
The belief that there are other
unnumbered universes occurring randomly
makes it necessary that time

now accommodate not just us,
but the origination and decay
of numberless universes,
a process with no prospect
of having had a beginning or of ever having an end.
So in addition to infinity, we must now also
take eternity seriously.
Try teaching this in Kansas.

Moving Clouds

When I was 40
and used to jog,
I had a neat way of telling
when I had stopped long enough
at the far end of my run.
It was when I had collected myself enough
to see that the clouds were moving.
This would take a minute or two,
sometimes longer if I was tired.
Then I would start back.
The clouds never moved
when I was running.

Sarah

When my daughter Sarah was six
I used to kneel beside her bed
and say some little prayer
or something quieting and good.
One night she said
Am I God?
I said, "Close,
the whole universe was made for you."
To this day I know it's true.
To this day I know it's true,
but I keep it to myself.

Sarah was the fastest runner
in her Junior High School class.
Now, my granddaughter Annika
is the fastest runner in hers.
Sarah says it must be in the jeans.
Why do these people make me weep?

My First Experiment

When I was six
My cousin Donny explained
how an electrical short happens.
He must have explained it well
because the next morning
I went down our street
to where there was an electric fence.
I found a piece of rotten board
still wet from last night's rain,
put one end in the mud,
the other against the wire.
And got shocked just like Donny said.
If it did this to me,
what would happen to a fly
if it landed on the board?
No flies were landing on my board.
So I spit on it.
Presently a fly landed near my spit,
fell over dead
and rolled down the board.
Just then the sun
made the edges of a small cloud incandescent;
a muddy kneed theophany.
That's when I became a scientist.

My Love-Life as a Kid

As a kid I was a little Romeo,
but it was all in my head and nostrils.
On the first day of kindergarten
I socked Maurice Pattingale.
Our sailor caps got mixed up
and all I could think of was to hit him.
Maurice had to sit by the blackboard
and I had to sit on Miss Johnson's lap
all through recess.
I was in love with Miss Johnson
and definitely unrepentant.
I did well in kindergarten.
In second grade I fell in love with Alice Kay
a blue-eyed vision that still haunts me.
Coming back from the boy's room
I would detour into the cloakroom
and sniff her coat. Long slow sniffs
that forged a special bond between us.
By the fourth grade
I was already managing to be the one next to her
so that we would hold hands in the Mayday Parade.
In the fifth grade, I confess,
one time when no one was looking,
I kissed her bicycle seat—
I thought you could probably be arrested for that.
By the sixth grade she was the prettiest thing on earth.
She agreed to go to a dance with me,
something I'd never done.

She had to show me
which arm to hold out.
That was embarrassing.
In the eighth grade
her mother got cancer and died.
That changed her happy personality.
It didn't help that her dad
right away married my dad's nurse, Evelyn.
Kay then developed some aloofness.
Despite that I idolize her to this day,
I quit pursuing her.
When I was a Junior,
Judy came along,
a bright, redheaded farm girl
that lived near Conway,
several miles from town.
She was a sophomore and had the neatest smile.
We had a few shy dates,
then one that rocked my world.
I took her in my mother's '41 Oldsmobile
to the McPherson Drive In Theater.
It started real slow
but we got to kissing
as though it was our last chance in life,
my heart going with its governor off,
and it kept up like this 'til my mouth was sore,
through the movie, the previews and the Goodnight Folks.
It's a wonder I could drive her home.
I must have sensed I was over my depth,
a boy messing with a woman.
I regret to say I stopped seeing her.
To this day I haven't experienced
anything quite like that again.
I've heard she's in a nursing home now
with severe dementia.
I dare not go to see her.

Sixty years later I apologized to Maurice Pattingale,
then a history professor at DU.
He said I was completely forgiven.
That's the only time I was ever completely forgiven.

Flirting

After reading Kathleen's essay on flirting
I thought, if I <u>do</u> that, it is certainly in a different way.
I just fall in love.
Like with this exquisite woman who fascinates me,
the one with the darting, musical eyes.
Indeed with such knowing, laughing eyes,
surely she can't realize how supernatural they are.
I'm so happy she comes to our meeting.
What I "do" is surely not flirting.
I simply adore her from wherever I'm sitting.
Whatever I do—laughing with her if she laughs,
studying her lovely eyes when she speaks,
responding to her as though she were a genie
directing my spirit (she is)—none of these require intention on my part.
The few things that require a little thought are:
I take it for granted that she is such a sensitive spirit
that she would not be impressed by anything obvious;
I make eye contact only furtively.
When it is my turn to speak,
I try to be intelligent and brief.
If she laughs, I smile in conspiracy.
I have not touched her and I would not unless invited.
The most flagrant thing I've said so far has been,
"I enjoyed what you said about…
I hope you come back."
But this restrained "flirting," if it is flirting,
surely has something to do with the fact
that we are both married

(and I expect, intend to stay that way),
of my being a good bit older,
but of thinking it would be wonderful
if she were half as fascinated with me
as I am with her. I also have to take into account
that a friend of mine recently said I amount
to an indefatigable fool. Truth can be helpful.

Claustrophobia

During a nap
I visualized my portion of infinity
the way I usually do:
a sprinkling of sand-size universes,
the dark infinite abyss beyond.
I was suddenly seized with panic:
How can I get out of here?
I'll find a way.

Beyond the Outermost Sphere

Aristotle conceived of a universe
of several concentric spheres.
But he could not conceive
of anything beyond the outermost sphere.
Why? He said it was because
there was no such thing as a vacuum,
no such thing as infinity.
Crescas thought these were
separate arguments and refuted them.
I too think a rather impious thought:
that this great man's elaborate, unconvincing
denial of vacuum and infinity
was *in order* not to believe
in something beyond the outermost sphere,
in something beyond himself.

A Volunteer Elm

There's a volunteer elm
that I'm watching grow
30 feet from my study window.
I've cut it down twice,
but this year let it grow.
A scarce five feet tall
when my wife left me
this summer to care for the cats,
houseplants and all
to be with her kin in west Texas.
I measure its growth
by my window slats.
Most mornings it's grown
upward half a slat.
Some mornings I can't see
a difference at all.
Maybe it's getting
thicker than tall.
Now that my wife's back
it's grown 14 slats,
fills half of the window,
filters the sun.
This tree and I
share a disposition.
We are equally concerned 'bout the world's rhetoric,
a barn that has burned,
what someone has earned,
or if I've been spurned
by a gossiping neighbor.

I water my tree
and we mainly consult
one another.

Necessary Field Work

Anita was our financial officer,
a tall spinster about 50.
As the field season was closing in '82
my project was running out of money.
In Anita's office, I made what appeals
I could, "just one last set of samples—"
I had to get them or lose a year's work.
I was desperate.
When all arguments were exhausted,
I said, confidentially,
Anita, if you'll put a thousand dollars
in my project,
I'll make love to you.
She shook her head
in what I thought was disappointment
but shuffled her papers
in such a way as to indicate
that the interview was over.
Next day I was xeroxing
when she came walking by.
When I smiled at her
she ran down the hall screaming
"Get away from me! Get away from me!"
Those nearby confirmed that all I had done
was smile.
But I got reprimanded for it anyway.
I paid for the field work myself.

Detachment *or*
How to Stay Married

Detach: L., *dis tache*, literally "un-nail"
to unfasten, separate, disconnect (O.E.D.)
In the best sense I acquire from Al-Anon literature,
detachment is to stay attached in certain essential
ways, but to maintain my equilibrium and poise by disengaging
emotionally, perhaps physically, from certain situations or behaviors.
I know that it is often convenient if not necessary to forget
that I am dependent on the fire department should my house catch fire,
that I am dependent on the drugstore for digoxin,
that when I plant a tree, I will not see it in its maturity.
that I can get lonely without her.
I can't function unless I forget these things sometimes.
In its short form,
detachment is to keep my hands off and my mouth shut.
In tense situations to make sparing use of my intelligence,
not to roll my eyes when she explains something.
To realize that most of my spontaneous comments
are a subtle form of control.
Not to provide a solution.
The essence of detachment with love
is to remember her devotion to me,
to be supportive and encouraging.
To remember I'm not the coach.
To relish her sensible conclusions,
to know that she too has a rescuing logic.
Except in life-threatening situations

not to warn her "for her own good."
It is to trust her God as well as my own.
When I am criticized or attacked
it is to concede what is true and not to defend myself.
A hostile diatribe is like excrement.
It is not improved by decoration.
It is to know that her anger hurts her more than me.
When she is sweet, to respond lovingly,
to offer to go for a walk, or just to sit together,
to take her out to eat, or watch a movie she likes.
When I find myself trapped, to find a quiet spot
and make a phone call or just reflect on the freedom
available in my own thoughts or at the next meeting.
It is to keep the Serenity Prayer handy,
to praise her for her courage and generosity,
for her resilience in the face of difficulty.
To reflect on my love for her,
and to express it in words and actions, often.

Overalls

When I was a kid
my dad left me to help out
on a Mennonite farm
at harvest time.
These folks were his patients.
That was in 1951,
I was almost thirteen.
One morning I went with their son Marlin
to take a truckload of wheat
to the Moundridge Mill.
When we turned into town
three girls in faded overalls
started skipping down the sidewalk
arm in arm, singing,
skips and bottoms synchronized.
I was dazzled, hypnotized.
I'd never seen overalls do that.
After we turned the corner
toward the mill
Marlin explained
that farm girls know how to
get into a pair of overalls.
I remember thinking,
Well, that's pretty obvious!
I've been parsing Marlin's sentence
now for sixty years…
and it's just not that obvious anymore.

Nevertheless, I've starting wearing overalls.
Sometimes I blush around farm girls.

The Anthropic Principle

The anthropic principle
as originally defined is that
theories of the universe
are constrained by man's
very existence in it as observers.
This principle is verified
by the history of cosmology,
which began with us being
the center of things.
Now it has come to the point
that we are the merest cipher
in an infinite system.
Quantum physics is now to the point
of concluding that all that
is observable, in fact all that can exist
is a necessary artifact
of infinite nothing.
And because any subset of an
infinite existent is infinite,
it is necessary to conclude
that there are an infinite number of
observers and reasoners like ourselves.
Is it not grounds for compassion
for an infinite number of

disappointed observers
who know the same thing?
Indeed compassion for ourselves?
At the very least
there is no room for arrogance.

The One Thing I Lack

I never had the courage
to be Jewish.
I never had sufficient passion.
The nearest I came to that passion
was a prayer of my own
that I be worthy
to reach out my hand
and pick up the prayerbook
so many have died to bring me.
I had the capacity to read Maimonides,
to go into a convulsion of repentance
reading the *Eight Chapter*s,
to have Bahya
as an intimate companion,
to have his living spirit
in the room with me.
In synagogues I saw
the inviolable holiness
of faces in prayer.
It was something I wanted,
but I was not part of it
except when alone.
When I was forty, I hit on the truth.
When I had been given
an international editorship
I realized I had most of what
I could wish for.
The one thing I lacked was

to have been born Jewish,
an opinion from which I've
not deviated.
But I've learned to be content.
A full measure of compunction
is mine,
and the great ones of the past
do not shun me.

The Impossibility of Shape

From childhood I learned to think
that everything had a shape,
the clouds, the earth, the galaxy,
the universe we can see.
But Giordano Bruno,
in considering the infinite void,
realized it can have no shape.
Somehow this is startling to me.
For instance, it cannot have
the shape of an infinite sphere
or any shape whatever,
because if it had any shape,
something would have to enclose it.
(This in fact was Aristotle's illogical
conclusion about the outermost sphere:
that it can have no enclosure of any kind,
that it is the limit of everything.)
Bruno believed in an infinite expanse
beyond the universe.
He realized that any shape whatever
would nullify
the essential feature of the abyss,
its omnidirectional infinity.
This appears to be the ungraspable notion,
that our enclosing abyss
is infinite in all directions.
And, incidentally,
has always existed. Always will.

For this, Bruno, a Dominican,
was burned at the stake.
Rabbi Hasdai Crescas,
who preceded Bruno in this opinion,
was bold enough to cryptically infer
that this infinite enclosure
was the God of the Talmud.

My God Concept

Indeed I have a God,
though others find it strange.
It is actually a single conception,
though it has parts.
One is ultimate,
that I will one day join
the infinite, eternal,
unknowable abyss itself,
the container
of finite universes.
The other, more useful,
I identify
as the equally unbelievable
human spirit,
the shared unconscious mind,
a habitat tailor-made for me.
More exactly, I think of it
as the "Zeppelin hangar"
my dad showed me
when I was eight.
That Zeppelin hangar
is now my unconscious mind,
the holder of my superego.
I refer only
to the Zeppelin hangar
in which I live.
I know I am entirely
in its hands.

Like Job I trust it
though it slay me.
Yes, I take my ballcap off
when others pray to theirs.

Death

My house has a breaker
in the furnace room.
I too am a low amp circuit
and have a breaker
in the furnace room.
The kindness of nature
has provided that
what I am and know
can never die.
Living is all I do.
This moving moment
is in a sense eternal.
I will not,
cannot, know
when the breaker trips.
Death is anyway
a small matter,
just a rumor,
nothing to do with me.

Are You Saved?

Just turned eight
I went to church alone
for some reason
and sat alone up front.
A young dark-haired usher
sidled up beside me,
put his arm around me
and asked in a whisper
"Are you saved?"
"Oh yes" I lied,
heart pounding.
He left me alone.
I've never gotten over that,
except to resolve
on a more militant answer.
In high school I began reading
critical theology and Freud.
I continued this in college
and throughout much
of my early lifetime.
At a certain point
I had the story,
one that is not yet publishable.
One, in fact,
that is criminal

if one considers
that the Athenian law
under which Diagoras of Melos
was hounded to death
is still in force.
It is.

My Motorcycle

Every time I leave the house
on my motorcycle
I know I may come back
in an ambulance,
dead or broken up.
I am in effect risking everything.
I know that and think of it
while riding.
Yet I do it.
Why?
It has something to do
with being alive,
with overcoming an old fear,
and though I am old,
with still being a man,
of passing other old men
on their big Harleys,
men who are possibly
gentlemen scholars,
who hold out a left arm to me.
I ride this thing because somehow
my dear wife and my conscience
let me.
This is not to deny that sometimes
I am aghast at myself.

My Old Friend

At seventy-four
I still have some moxie left.
Despite the prediction of rain,
I put on my rain gear
and rode two hours
through the mountains
to meet my old friend.
Each year our wives approve
our spending two days together.
The most interesting thing
about this visit
is that he, in effect, remakes me.
He is more fascinated by me
than I am.
I return the same attention.
We seldom interrupt one another,
and we remember
what the other one says.
We tell each other difficult truths.
He will encourage me
to recite a poem to him.
If I shed tears
so does he.
Where else
could I find
such a friend?

What a Good Woman Deserves

A woman who devotes herself
to a man
deserves to be worshiped.
She offers all she has
in return for the board
she would sleep on.
She would fight and die
for the uncouth nothing
that may scorn her,
mock her,
and never, ever
be worthy of her.

A Woman's Life

The unavoidable affliction
of a woman's life,
it seems to me,
is the necessity
to be attractive to men.
Those who are not
and not able to compensate
can suffer terribly.
This is why
the prayer book says
Blessed art thou
O Lord our God…
who hast not made me
a woman.

PTSD Explained

What is now called PTSD
--in Sigmund Freud and Joseph Breuer's studies, the master work on it—
was called hysteria.
It consists of a profound insult
inadequately responded to
at the time.
What can cure or change
the symptoms—often fear
of similar situations—
is reliving that situation
and adequately responding to it.
In my case it started with
a motorcycle wreck in 1973.
It gave me horrid nightmares
when I wanted another.
I gave up the idea and it
deterred the nightmares and fear.
But thirty-six years later, inspired,
I rebuilt two motorcycles
and rode them, full of fear.
I bought a third one new
and ride it a lot.
I still have an occasional
useful fearful imagining,
but I no longer have nightmares.
Now I'm beginning to have fun.

Maurine

One day thirty years ago
I became aware
of a flaming redhead
sitting on a stool
with her legs crossed,
way too sure of herself.
I didn't know
what to make of her.
But when I learned
she would pick up
two men at once,
drink 'til
no bar would serve her,
was actually kicked out of a *town* in California,
And now is forty years sober,
a temple of compassion—
I knew she was a goddess.
Now I'm devoted
to the shadow she casts.
I love her with my soul.

The Infinite Abyss and Me

The infinite abyss
has no shape.
(If it did, something
would have to surround it.)
It has no middle
or it would have to have ends.
Who could tell where those would be?
There are no directions in the abyss,
no up or down,
north or south.
In a region infinitely far
from any identifiable thing,
it would be impossible
to speak of circular
or rectilinear motion
both of which
require a reference.
In the infinite depths
of the abyss there can be
no orientation whatever.
Nor, it seems to me,
could one speak of time.
Could the ubiquitous innumerable
minuscule universes throughout
simply be futile rebellions
against this infinite Nothingness?
Rebellions against
its incomprehensible vastness?

Yet Rabbi Hasdai Crescas,
a 14th-century cosmological seer,

makes the comforting assertion
that space is one,
its dimensions immutable.
That is, despite being infinite
with no shape,
it is a definite, unchanging place,
any particular point of which
is and always has been perdurably fixed.
Despite there being no reference,
nowhere to drive in a surveyor's stake,
despite the impossibility of triangulation,
or a 'GPS',
one must believe
that every location, every point in the void,
is immovable forever.
Somehow, the infinite Nothing
is a definite, substantial constant
that does not move,
that can be trusted to have been the same,
to stay the same forever.
For a brief moment
Hasdai thought
this must be God.
Could it be that some
recalcitrant proton of mine
might stray into and, Void forbid,
contaminate this holy space?

Untitled

Of adultery
the Dhammapada says
"…brief is the joy
of the frightened man and woman."
What could be more true?
But there is a better sort
of adultery,
if one could call it that.
Far more adult.
It is an unintended,
righteous passion
deep in the heart;
an attachment
that can persist forever,
unblemished.
The sadness it may occasion
is outweighed
by the sustenance
of something
steady and beautiful.

Laughter

The hermit poet Tao Yuan-Ming
and a Ch'an Buddhist friend,
a monk,
are said one day to have visited
Hui-yuan, a famous scholar
who lived alone
on a mountain.
The three of them
went for a walk
in the valley.
Crossing the bridge
over the Tiger River,
they heard a lone tiger roar.
These holy men
looked at one another
and laughed.
So loved were they
by the people,
that on the place
where they laughed
a temple was erected
to commemorate their laughter.

Adapted from Robert Payne's *White Pony* (1947; p.152)

Fidelity

When we've had wonderful sex
My wife may whisper
"That was wonderful, dear."
I may sometimes whisper back
"That's what all the girls say."
She'll smile.
She knows I couldn't say that
if it were true.

An Abandoned Farm

Doing fieldwork in Nevada
forty years ago
near a back road
twenty miles from nothing,
I found an abandoned farm.
Big trees where they ought not to be.
What once must have been
a barn, a shed,
a three-room house
of never-painted wood,
not yet quite fallen down.
There must have been
a wife and children,
a son gone off to war?
Is that a little seesaw stand
poking through the boards?
the shreds of a sandbox there
beside that dead branch perfect
for a swing?
They all bespeak
a father's gentle love.
I could understand
great grandchildren thinking
'he's now up above this place,
it's really not abandoned.'

The brave labor of that ruin
still haunts and stabs me
like a verse from Ecclesiastes;
the brave labor of human dreams!
Those boards still speak to me.

Bahya

Bahya,
that great human heart,
furnace of brotherly love.
Like me,
he must have wandered blind,
studying, searching.
He knew the Talmud,
revered Aristotle.
One place in the *Duties*
shows that he knew
the Gospel of Matthew,
another place shows that he knew
the bawdiest of bawdy poetry,
the Greek Anthology.
Was it because of a free-thinking past
that he became
such a furnace of piety?
He didn't show me,
he demonstrated God.
His night-time prayers
embarrass me,
but I read them when I can—which is not often.
What I most remember of Bahya
is when he catches his breath,
reaches out his hand
and says, "Oh, my brother…"
Here I feel God.

Going to Church

This Sunday
I'm going to church,
even though it's against
my principles.
There's no way out of it.
After years of being too sick,
my wife is playing the organ.
I may be an atheist
according to them,
but I'm not a knave.
I might even hum the hymns
and seem respectable.
I'll listen carefully
for the train whistle.

Atheists

I was taught as a lad
that the only thing
infinite and eternal
is God.
The multiverse hypothesis
has the unanticipated effect
of requiring one to conceive
of the infinite, empty space
in which universes occur:
there is thus an unstoppable
algebraic equation:
whatever over infinity
is zero.
If there were a dense cluster
of universes, say, $10^{1,000,000}$ light years across,
filling all we can imagine,
it would still be finite
in every dimension,
zero in the Great All.
So at the scale of true infinity,
true eternity,
all the universes we can imagine
are infinitely small,
infinitely brief.

Thus according to God
we do not exist.
So much for atheists.

A Woman's Eyes

I've just begun to realize
that what runs the world
are a woman's eyes.
They guide large vessels
with visible sighs,
their magical, mystical rudder.
One mischievous glance
like an earthquake perchance,
can topple whole cities down.
How is it I never saw this before,
that those animate eyes,
heaven's loose door,
can zap the flintiest reason.

What Should a Man Think?

Given the new probability,
in fact, the inevitability
of 'infinite' universes,
minuscule in infinite space,
of an eternity
that makes our moment
disappear,
what happens to our heroes,
in those secret places of the spirit?
To Leonidas, to Socrates,
Aristotle and Hillel?
Galileo and Stephen Hawking?
to Rosa Parks, who wouldn't sit
in the back of the bus?
Do they all go away
with proton decay?
Or is their spirit a music
that will never die?
Something equal
to the dark abyss we live in?
Concerning the certainty
of our Planck-length space,
of the eternity our moment
is part of,
what should a man think

looking out at the stars?
What should he do?
Feed a stray cat?
Give two dollars to a homeless man?
Maybe weep
for what seems to be God?

The Way My Father Walked

Did the way my father walked
amount to a manifesto
to his Isle of Man
preacher father?
It was a more-than-manly stride
a clomping, stooped-forward
virile stride,
as unquestionable
as though he was intending,
three steps away,
to pick up a fallen child.
It was a stride safe
in the face
of sacerdotal criticism.
I've always thought
that was the way
a man should walk.
But I seldom feel entitled
to walk that way myself.

To a Vulture

Does not that lowly vulture,
sitting on a limb,
display enormous dignity
praying for his kin
to have a peaceful death?

Does the vulture smile at eagles,
who risk their life and limb
to seem more fine and noble,
than their unimpressive kin
content with ignominy?

So is our lowly vulture
a philosopher in a tree
contemplating life and death
and true humility?
Who would guess?

Skylark thou never wert—

Happiness

No matter if I'm suff'ring
from a bruising 'spite the buffering
of a cheerful padded brain,
it just stimulates inventiveness
and lasts a little while.
And there's always something
laughy, something piquant,
salty, sappy,
to make me reasonably happy
if I think on it a while.
If I catch a case of ho-hums
wracked with ennui, horrid
doldrums,
there's a way for me
to compensate
and hope for something swell.
Even if I were sentenced
to Dostoevsky's shelf,
I think I could be stolid
and kindly to myself
just by reflecting
Hallelujah, I'm alive.

Return

To a perfectly dark
infinite vacuum
with no shape,
no boundaries,
no end or direction,
no up or down,
seemingly no time,
no sound,
no here or there,
no way to explore it,
only widely scattered
particle happenings,
only the rarest
of opportunities
for infinitely distant,
falsifiably existent
theoretical physicists.
I will return
and rest
for a sizeable
subeternity again;
I will joyfully return,
happy there 'til I do it again
after who knows
how long a time.
Then joyfully return
to another here,
perhaps a better poet.

Darwin's Brother

Darwin's peculiar brother,
Erasmus,
left an immortal saying:
"I find the *a-priori* method
so satisfactory that,
if the facts don't agree,
so much the worse
for the facts."
I tend to practice this myself.

More on the Size of Things

What awes me, what I can't seem
to get out of my head
is where we are with respect to what is.
If our galaxy (100,000 light years across)
were the size of a shirt button,
and we were to scale everything accordingly,
the farthest the Hubble Space Telescope can see
(some 13 billion light years hence)
would be 10 miles from our shirt button galaxy.
Current estimates are
that the actual edge of our universe is
at least ten,
probably many times more, that far away.
But even the ten-fold minimum allows
a startling, attention-getting scale calculation.
With respect to our button,
the volume of our (visible) toy universe
is a little over 4,000 cubic miles.
If the edge of our universe is
even 10 times further out,
its volume would be
a little over 4,000.000 cubic miles.
This being the minimum guess,
what we can see is a mere thousandth part—almost certainly less—
of the universe around us.
Even compared to our galaxy button,
the universe would appear to be
incomparably bigger than we thought.

And the best guess now
is that there are an infinite number of universes
like this and not like this
throughout an infinite void,
with only a tiny, yet infinite subset
that will support life.
God seems to have thrown an infinite number of dice
to come up with a mere infinite number of us.
Believing physicists today say that strings are absolutely fundamental,
there being nothing smaller…
But wouldn't the points from which they originate be more fundamental,
and more fundamental than the fathering vacuum?

My Life as a String

In 2063
astronomers on earth noticed
that a well-known galaxy
near their visible cosmic horizon
had disappeared.
When other nearby galaxies
rapidly began to disappear
it became clear
that a massive black hole
was eating them
and soon the whole visible universe
and the invisible extension adjacent
would be next.
It happened that I was ahead of them,
having accelerated
through the event horizon,
as luck would have it, unharmed,
being not quite as small a string as one can get.
My great grandfather
was a piece of microscopic space debris,
my grandfather a proton somewhere within,
my father a happy-go-lucky quark.
(None of us had mothers.)
Then there was me,
a little string half a Planck length long.
Or so I've heard.
These progenitors were still whizzing
relativistically toward where a lot of everything

then was—this unbelievably massive black hole,
some 10 billion light years
into the center of their previously visible universe.
By the time I reached the event horizon,
I was already zero dimensional,
one of maybe 10 to the google to the google
to the google to the google to the google
of other dimensionless points of energy,
packed into this by now universe-sized black hole.
So that's how things began for me,
as a dimensionless point,
at an indefinite location,
an imaginary, non-existent location
that did not have
any comforting,
theoretical dimensions.
We points are said to be spawns of the infinite vacuum,
our preferred mythology,
scattered like tiny chunks of chicken
in an infinite chicken soup.
Somewhere, who knows where,
inside this black hole
we assembled in enormous crowds
and did as we pleased
beneath the imagined surface
of adult stringhood,
the dreaded Planck length,
10^{-29} microns, one of the 100 billion billion billion
diminutive stretches hidden in a millimeter.
We thought of this length
as a crime-scene police line,
like Baptists think of sin:
an unforgivable trespass
you don't want to get started in.
I had for a long time been safe
as a non-existent point,

but, a quantum physics thing,
I reached adolescence.
Every now and then
I became one entire dimension,
but thankfully, quite as non-existent as previously.
But I liked it when stretched out, non-existently slim
(no wider that the non-existent point I started from).
I was aware of having lost
a huge amount of energy
in having become a line.
Then, from wherever I was,
(quantum physics again),
I approached the dreaded Planck length,
and instinctively recoiled.
Somehow I knew that if I broke though the Planck length,
I would lose vast amounts of energy, becoming real, acquiring
gross thickness and a specifiable length.
It was scary. But I did it, couldn't help it.
Only breaking though just a little bit,
I desperately turned back,
seeking my earlier non-existent self.
But as I began to turn,
suddenly I acquired an unwanted second dimension,
and not only that, but a brief taste of subjection
to the tyranny of the physical constants,
an inescapable oligarchy, the large and small forces,
the electromagnetic thing, and least and worst of all, gravity,
which is no joke in a black hole.
Ducking this danger, I turned back in terror,
seeking without thought my other end,
trying again to become a nonexistent point.
But I had lost too much energy to shrink.
I could hardly think. I was irreversibly corrupted.
I first became a disreputable two-dimensional loop.
Then, still mindless, I grasped my other end
and became a circle, terribly confused about where to think I am.

Things were suddenly getting crowded.
But getting used to the confusion, I began to hum,
a sort of mindless metronomic hum,
then to keep time with my humming,
my non-existent circumference began bopping in and out.
So here I was, a non-existent circle bopping around by myself.
Well, bingo again, it caught on. There was a teenage
would-be superstring melee in a black hole 3-D disco.
Unfortunately we were infiltrated
just then by far more numerous, supremely energetic
non-existent points that couldn't dance.
We jeered at them, derisively, called them
zero-dimensional sex-police.
They were upset by our music,
particularly our circumferential vibrations,
which they declared to be
two-dimensionally obscene.
A general panic ensued.
It had to do just then,
with the catastrophic collapse
of our giant black hole.
We were getting squeezed
like you wouldn't believe.
What happened was that we started losing our
one and two dimensions,
with a great increase of energy.
We were for an instant all super-energetic points again,
condensing into equally non-existent lumps.
Then the lumps congealed and we became
one non-existent point,
an unimaginably energetic, dimensionless singularity
containing who-knows-how-many universes.
The lot of us then exploded through the Planck length
and kept growing super-luminously, ignoring symmetry,
becoming whatever chance would have us be,
in an inflationary spray of new universes.

But it must be said, in modesty,
in the larger scheme of things,
the noise (if you could call it that)
was like a small raindrop
hitting a fluffy sheepskin. Yes, it was inaudible.
But anthropically lucky astronomers
may someday call it a Big Bang.
One must wonder if all those unfulfilled
high-energy, non-existent points
that inflated outward laughing,
at some exponential multiple of the speed of light,
those unfulfilled would-be strings, now
everywhere-detectable ghost-like things,
are what puzzle us as dark matter and dark energy.
Who knows? We will see.

Dan

I'm going to lose my friend Dan.
Without knowing each other
we used to drink in the same bars
on the other side of the state.
Then we sobered up and moved here.
We didn't like each other at first,
but that changed.
Now we always sit together.
For three years now
through every exigency
his tumors have been kept in abeyance.
Now they're everywhere
and there's nothing to be done.
His looks have changed.
He's lost twenty pounds.
Yesterday we had lunch,
talked about cars and motorcycles.
As we parted, he said
he intended to skip some pain pills
and go for a ride.
That stabbed me.
Without thinking, I said
"Don't be a martyr."
I hope he understood.

What I meant was
"Please don't endure
unendurable pain
just to ride
that motorcycle."

Dan's Legacy

After his battle with cancer
a well-meaning neighbor asked Dan
"Would there be any harm
now in drinking?
Surely you know that you can."
After a moment's reflection,
Dan managed to help him see.
"Why would I want to stop being the man
I've always wanted to be?"
That thought's become a theme with me,
I think of it now as Dan's legacy,
to die the man I've wanted to be,
the man I've always wanted to be.
Dan helped me to be that man.

My Last Breakfast with Dan

One morning last summer
I waited for Dan at the Philips station.
He rolled in on his Darth Vader Spyder,
led the way through town,
out Hwy 92 and up Hwy 65 through Cedaredge
to the Bakery Cafe.
We sat outside in the sun
on the corner of the deck.
After breakfast,
Dan smoked and told me
such an embarrassing thing
that happened 50 years ago.
It was the first time he'd told it.
I loved him for it.
I blushed and confessed
I didn't have anything that good to tell.
He paid the bill.
On the way back I was in the lead.
At Hwy 92, while I was accelerating
for all my 250 was worth.
Dan came rocketing past me,
with a small Darth Vader smile I bet.
Of course he had to slow down
so I could catch up.
We behaved like gentlemen

the rest of the way to Delta.

He waved goodbye at the Stafford stoplight.

Two days ago he stopped breathing.

He's still rocketing past me.

It's Me

I've always been a modest man,
doing what I think I can,

I put an edge upon my hoe,
and cut the weeds or let them grow,
wearing an old sweater.

I'll read Spinoza late at night,
always thinking "Well, he's right…
but maybe I know better."

What 'er I do I know is good;
I never use the phrase "I should."
After all, it's me.

I love my little neighborhood,
each summer it is understood
we'll have a backyard party.

We'll all talk about the food,
the absent neighbor's nasty mood.
I never mention Alfarabi.

I spend the evenings here alone
helping Sisyphus with his stone;
then we laugh and let the damn thing lie.

I am such a noble beast
I'll be buried facing east
riding this colossus
at a thousand miles an hour.
After all, it's me.

Even I

If I should approach
the eternal abyss,
the, infinite, shapeless abyss
and somehow remember
Pachelbel's Canon,
the Moonlight Sonata,
or the last stirring part of Beethoven's Fifth,
I'd know even I
who hardly exist
would not have lived for nothing.
I'd know I'd not have lived for nothing.

Life

I'm entranced with thee,
with every creature I see,
with my wife, my neighbor,
my grandchildren three.
This is such an emotional time for me,
I'm in love with my life,
with eternity,
with writing maudlin poetry.
'Twas a careless life
so sad to see,
But I'd do it all over again.

The Assembly of Life

If one plots the abundance
of elements in sea water
according to their natural occurrence
in the volume of one cubic micrometer—the average volume of bacteria—
one finds that the cobalt ion
is the heaviest central-chart ion
for which at least one ion occurs
in this volume.
This is apparently the break point
for metallic ions immediately available
to the first bacteria-sized organisms
to have assembled in sea water.
(There is evidence that the composition
of sea water has been stable long enough
for this conclusion.)
There are only a few odd elements
heavier than cobalt that have any use
in either the metabolism or structure
of living organisms today.
What does this mean?
It means that the earliest self-replicating
oceanic life forms
assembled according to the relative
abundance of elements
in the average volume of the sea water
they inhabited.
It is thus no coincidence that
the elements in use in all organisms today

(with the few exceptions mentioned)
are elements lighter than cobalt.
All elements heavier than cobalt
are increasingly toxic to terrestrial
and oceanic forms—the heavier
and rarer, the more toxic.
This trend can be demonstrated
by plotting the binding constants
of the elements with essential proteins
containing cysteine.
The heavier and rarer the element
in seawater,
the more tightly it binds to the essential
proteins in protective membranes.
A consequence of this is that oceanic bacteria
are all, in effect, soldiers for each other,
scooping up ions according to their toxicity,
protecting others.
Oceanographers have found
that a constant rain of bacterial detritus
occurs throughout the oceans,
especially in quiet areas near eastern
shorelines, as near the coast of Peru.
According to what we have found,
this bacterial detritus, progressively
enriched in metals heavier than cobalt,
will have been salting the soon to be
subducted sediments for the last few
billion years of life in the oceans.
The process that results in
magmatic ore deposits has thus
for a few billions of years
been inheriting sediments with metals
whose abundances are,
so curiously to many geologists,
about inversely proportional to their

terrestrial and oceanic occurrence.
Tellurium, for instance,

that occurs at the part per billion level or less
in crustal rocks, is found in the parts per million level
and higher around the volcanogenic Ely deposit.
How did that happen? I think we know.
Most if not all terrestrial ore deposits
are biogenic, absolutely consonant
with the way life formed in the oceans.

A Drinking Dream

I haven't had a drinking dream
for a year, the one where I captured
six hundred gallons of vodka.
But I had one before I woke this morning.
The details are not that sketchy.
I was with the little sister
I've been in love with since I was ten
but never touched.
We were in a storage room
where a twenty-gallon jug had fallen over
and was still rocking, pouring out
little pulses and drips of wine
into the sink underneath,
maybe the cold Carlo Rossi white wine
that used to be my staple.
What a waste!
It was easy to fill a plastic water glass,
taste it just to see what it was—though I knew,
then drink it down, the whole glass,
the whole full water glass full.
I was instantly half drunk.
I rummaged in a cupboard
for one of the half-liter brandy snifters
I used to drink from,
While it was filling, I began to think
"I've had a whole water glass of wine
and there's nothing I can do about it now.
After twenty-six years

I will have to raise my hand
and be a newcomer,

raise my hand for thirty days,
a terrible dilemma.
But I knew I had drunk
that whole glass of wine
and couldn't do anything about it now.
Then, praise God, I awoke.
After a cup of coffee now
I realize why that dream was.
I have been in love
with a blonde-headed beauty
like my sister—whom I have touched and desired,
and to whom I have voiced my feeling;
yet now have relinquished.
I violated my conscience
in words with her.
I've been sad and glad
for 'giving her up'
now for two days.
This proves to me
what a friend has said:
that a woman can be
the same as a drink.
And it occurs to me
that the poetry I've been writing
must be some kind of substitute
for drinking.
That's why it's been so good!

Growing Old

I still think of 'growing old'
as remote and far from me,
theoretic speculation
as far as I can see,
a predicate for others
in robust company,
not something any one of us
would yet say of ourselves.
But when a single month begins
with the death of three good friends,
all of whom were younger,
the speculation tends to linger,
a close and overfriendly
demonstration.

Reading a Prayer

Reading a prayer
to a dying woman
I had just taken through the Steps
was difficult.
She was patient
when I had to stop
at every few words
and struggle for composure.
When I read
"How goodly are thy tents
O Jacob, thy tabernacles,
O Israel!"
I could hardly continue.
When I read
"O Lord our God,
King of the universe…"
my face was wet,
I couldn't even breathe.
I didn't know
there was such passion
in those words.

My Three-Day Rule

Maimonides said that a sage,
before he carry out any act,
will consider well
whether it will be
consistent with the highest goal,
and only then will do it.
To my regret
I often do not do this.
But when I do,
in important matters,
I observe a three-day rule.
If after three days
I have no objection
to what I have said or planned,
I consider my response okay.
If after three days something
still troubles me,
I'll inventory it systematically,
maybe consult someone
and acknowledge my error,
sometimes not.
If I can carry out this rule
assiduously,
it stands me in good stead.
But as you see,
I don't follow this with poetry.

The Saint, the Sage, and the Alcoholic

Some maintain that the man without desire of the forbidden
is superior to the man with desires who restrains himself.
The Rabbis, however, say the opposite,
that he who craves iniquity (and yet does not do it)
is far more praiseworthy and perfect.
Rabbi Simeon ben Gamaliel, that sage of sages, in fact said
"[A] man should not say
'I do not want to eat meat together with milk;
I do not want to wear clothes made of a mixture of wool and linen;
I do not want to enter into an incestuous marriage…'"

Gamaliel anticipated Freud by fifteen hundred years.
A man is far better off accepting and making friends
with his unconscious mind than one duped by denial.
A man is better off admitting to himself and a closed-mouth friend
that he desires his neighbor's wife, than one who would deny it.
An overeater is better off admitting his endless desire for food
than one for whom that desire is a treacherous secret to be broken.
A matter of life and death is the case of a recovering alcoholic:
He should not say "I no longer have any desire to drink,"
but rather "I have a permanent unconscious desire to drink,
which I shall have 'til the day I die, (though I also now have
the opposite, an unconscious desire not to drink).
If he ignores the Big Book and claims
to be immune from drinking,
he is on the edge of a precipice.

The Destination

Most people think
they will go to their reward.
I too will go to mine.
I will be subsumed
in infinite darkness,
the infinite, silent abyss
where there is no time,
no shape, no up or down,
infinite nothingness,
a place of dreamless sleep.

Gerri Ellen

"To know Gerri Ellen is to hate her"
was a quip in the club house where we met.
No one could match her razor-sharp sarcastic wit.
She was a Harley-riding, needle-using,
suicidal New York Jewish girl.
She never touched anyone
but the thug that she was doing.
She only loved her two pit bulls.
When she got cancer, miracle of miracles,
she gave up alcohol and drugs,
and of all unexpected things,
told me I was her sponsor.
None of the women she'd asked were willing.
Amazingly my wife approved.
Scary? Ha! But she was ready.
So we quickly took the steps. She wrote them out,
told me her darkest secrets, made amends by letter.
One may have been accepted.
She started reading an orthodox prayer book of mine—she'd never seen one.
She started being nice to other alcoholics.
When the steps were done the cancer took over.
Her assignment was to "Hug people,
tell them that you love them."
She started with me
and I found I had to say "I love you" back.
When she had a short time to live,
one day she talked of dying
and said, "I know you'll see me through it,"

as though I were her rabbi. I'll never forget it.
When she had just weeks to live,
I'd visit if she'd call,
go there and read prayers to her;
but would have to stop
where my crying interfered.
I too was learning to love.

To Grasp Infinity

More than once
it has occurred to me
I'm not equipped
to grasp infinity
of either space or time.

If I cannot grasp
eternity, infinity as such,
does it really matter much
if I'm certain that they are?

So grasping what I can't conceive
confers a humble certainty,
a certain knowledge of infinity
I didn't know I had.

Thinking the unthinkable
is all I really have.

Recovery

Thank you O God,
whatever you are,
my Zeppelin hangar,
or a distant star
that is really a galaxy
of over a hundred billion.

The pain
of my Frankenstein staples
is a small price to pay
for my gratitude
to the cheerful young surgeon
who saved my life
a week ago today.

How grateful I am
for the friends
and their cards,
all signed with love,
who came up stairs
to see me.

How glad I am
not to be awakened
from a short nap
to have blood drawn
from my macerated arm.
For a wife

to supervise
my pathetic flirting
with the young beauties
who took care of me.
but mostly for a cup of coffee
made by me
to my own specifications,
that I can sip
here in the dark,
safe from that phlebotomist.
For my friends, my wife,
the salvage of my little life,
such as it is,
For the darling little nurse
who had to hug me good bye,
I am grateful.
for getting to know you,
O God,
a little better.

Theoretical Interest

A decrepit old woman's
in love with me.
I'm kind and nice as I can be.
When she offers to take a nap with me
I don't let it get out of hand.

Maybe it can be the same with us.
I'll be the ancient blunderbuss,
restraining myself, avoiding fuss,
and we both can observe decorum.

The bargain will be that you humor me,
though the love in my eyes
will be plain to see.
Your only risk is my poetry,
some of which you'll love.
And that won't bother me at all.

Abdominal Surgery

Often the smallest hit
will finish off a man.
Was this mine?
Vomiting up that nose tube—the most violent thing
since my drinking days?

I've always lived by haphazard,
but it's always seemed to do.
Now it's got to be Aristotle again,
looking over wisdom's edge,
following wise intuition
like Socrates again.

No more what the hell,
No more rebel yell,
no more passing semis
on that little motorcycle.

Damn! I'd rather be
like Slim Pickens
riding down that bomb
in a final ecstasy,
knowing, dear God,
that you'll remember me.
But probably not.

How Far Can We See?

The grandfather theorist of inflation,
Alan Guth, estimates that our actual universe
extends 10^{23} times further out than
the Hubble telescope can see
(13.75 billion light years).
I believe this is now
an almost universally accepted estimate.
If we assume it is right, all we need in order to get
the *ratio* between the Hubble distance
and the actual size of the universe
of which we are a part,
is to divide the Hubble distance by 10^{23}.
That will give us the relative scale.
If my arithmetic is right
that comes out to be eight tenths of a mile.
So the distance the Hubble telescope can see,
is as eight tenths of a mile to
the Hubble distance itself,
(which in our toy model we have set
to stand for the "edge"
of the actual universe itself.)
Eight tenths of a mile is not very far
in comparison to the Hubble distance.
But that may give some idea
of the microscopic part we can see

in relation to the size of our actual universe.
The ratio is the same
as the volume of a volley ball
to the volume of the earth.

Unacceptable Ideas

I learned by myself
as a younger, stupider man
that there are certain understandings
not wisely voiced.
Such ideas have always fascinated me,
urged me on, as it were,
to understand them as best I can,
to know the difference between certain truths
and acceptable understandings.
This fascination has become
much of my blessing, much of my curse.
For the same length of time
I've gradually seen the reason for this:
that certain understandings, if accepted,
would destroy the fabric of society,
produce mass hysteria.
There are historical instances of mass hysteria.
A fun example was when Zurich university
offered David Strauss a professorship,
and the people of Zurich rioted
—so that his professorship had to be dissolved
and Strauss "retired" with a pension.
Just as certain ideas cannot be accepted,
others cannot be discarded.
Thankfully, there are also certain ideas
that by their nature elude the common grasp,
for example, that death is final.
What I like is the ridiculous smallness

of our Hubble volume
in relation to the inevitable size
of our entire universe,
let alone that other unnumbered universes
necessarily exist,
that the void beyond is primordial, ultimately cold,
dark, empty, shapeless, infinite, eternal,
especially eternal.
Such an idea, now necessarily true,
is so ungraspable and useless,
as not even to be rumored on Main street.
Imagine the barber telling his customers!
This more or less constant soliloquy,
a happy meditation in the dark,
I safely share with friends who smile politely.
My friend Giordano is listening.

Dissonance

If I could lose
this queasy feeling
and relax
and take it easy,
if the dissonance could go,
would it be like silent snow
drifting in the dark
unimpeded?
If I could wrap myself in fog
and lose this agitation
that like some friendly dog
is always craving my attention,
I'd be at heaven's gate,
I wouldn't mind the wait.
I'd float like an eagle
on the music from within.
I'd know I was already
being smiled upon by God.

A Leaf

After some cosmological hype
My friend Charles Liston
suggested to me
to pull in my horns
and begin to see
how even a leaf
that's falling free
can just as easily
be thought to be
a Big Bang
offered by a tree.
This helps me retreat—incredibly!—
to one day,
one leaf
at a time.

Love Song

I love you, Honey.
I love the peace.
Your faults are your perfection.
Where 'er I go, what 'er I do,
I do with your affection.
And when I come
back home bereft, you lie beside me
there to lay your dear warm head
upon my chest
and float my cares away.
Yes, I love you, Honey.
I marvel at the things I see
drifting through the galaxy,
yet safe and warm as I can be.
Then wake an hour later, blest
your head yet snug upon my chest.
You fix coffee, maybe tea.
We sit and read a book 'til three
and laugh and talk it over,
to maybe once or twice dispute
some wrong pronunciation.
Wherever lost in space I am,
in dark infinity,
I know it's my creation, just,
vast as it may be.

So it's my muse, my last request,
perhaps someday to join it,
bathed in your tranquility,
approaching God, infinity,
your head upon my chest.
I so love you, Honey.

Gerri Ellen

When I first met Gerri Ellen
she was mad as hell and
hated everyone without exception.
Somehow she let me hug her,
let me tell her that I loved her.
I guess she knew I'd been that way myself.
After she got cancer and had blown off her last sponsor,
she asked around and sadly found not a soul to want her.
So when I took her home one night, she told me, "You're my sponsor."
Steps 1, 2, 3 were quickly past,
her 4th and 5th astonished me.
She told me stuff she'd never told before.
6, 7, 8, 9, 10; no great luck with her amends.
Hatred's so persistent in badly scalded friends.
Gerri was a New York Jew, an apostate through and through,
but it just so happens, too, Judaism's my salvation.
Her main assignment for 11 and 12 was to hug most everyone,
then tell them that she loved them—something that she did.
She practiced first on me. I'd just say mechanically
"Okay, come and hug me, tell me that you love me,"
the which she would obediently do.
I'd find I'd have to answer 'Gerri Ellen I love you.'
With her too sick to keep on trying,
I read her prayers despite my crying
that made the prayer book wet and made the reading hard.
Without coaching, then, she hugged me,
told me that she loved me,
and this time it wasn't an assignment.

Has this time with Gerri Ellen
been something that I dreamed.?
When I think of her
I know I've been redeemed.

My Neighbor George

My neighbor George, across the street,
always seems composed and neat,
friendly as any man could be.
On weekends he'll wave and greet
me if I'm working in the yard.
He has a sense of humor too.
Once spraying weeds, he stopped and said
"My needs are few; sometimes I need a laxative."
He told me thirty years ago he had some woman trouble,
nearly knocked him off his feet. A lead pipe cinch
he'll not repeat a dern fool thing like that again.
He gets up at three I guess,
anyway his lights are on, TV flicker and the rest.
I watch his lights through blinds I've drawn
with a mug of coffee. I'm always glad to be on time
to see his lights go out—five thirty-eight or five thirty-nine, precisely.
Then he backs his pickup out—at
five forty-one or five forty-two,
almost as good as a pulsar,
and heads down for breakfast
with Frank, Ed and Stew.
They talk and laugh a long, long time.
I know because I've been there while they're eating.
He's in the county shop at nine,
county trucks all in a line, awaiting his attention.
At five he'll head back home again
maybe get some groceries then
park his truck and wave again

if I'm outside in the yard.
I've heard our neighbors all aver–
George is friendly, patient, kind,
a small-town philosopher.
He keeps his roses fertilized,
often watered, neatly trimmed,
far more beautiful than mine.

The Bone Yard

How does an elephant know
when it's time to go
to the bone yard?
And never having been there,
can he be aware
of where it is?
(We won't suppose that he can tell, simply by the smell
of his kinfolk wafting off to heaven.)
If that location's random circumstance,
can genetic knowledge have a chance
of explaining how he knows just where it is?
Or has some other elephant shared this information?
Told him, "when you're ready follow me,"
or, "all you do is walk in that direction."
"You'll know when it comes time,
you'll see the reason and the rhyme,
and they may not even notice your defection."
So the bone yard's my last plan,
getting there, I think I can.
All I have to do is walk in that direction.
I doubt there'll be distraction,
I'll find perfect satisfaction
settling into place among my kin.
So I conclude it's not that hard
to know when or why or where
to join the other elephants
already there, in the bone yard.

Jean Valjean

When I was twelve
my father took me to the only movie,
he ever took me to—the first film version of Les Misérables.
The only thing that impressed me
was that my father had taken me to a movie.
I liked the escape from the galley.
When it came to the part
where the priest said to the officers,
"I gave him the candlesticks,"
my father had to catch his breath
and wipe his eyes.
I'd never seen him do that.
But that's the kind of man he was,
a repentant Jean Valjean,
though I doubt he'd ever stolen a loaf of bread.
So I've been reading that massive novel
all my life, always weeping at the part
where the priest says
"I gave him the candlesticks."

The Tomcat and the Blizzard

Something got me up an hour ago.
It wasn't the raging blizzard
or even the stinging snow
blowing in our bedroom window.
It was my bonny little wife
fretting 'bout the life of our tomcat.
To the back door she would go
in the wind and howling snow,
crying endlessly "Here Kitty, kitty, kitty!"
She kept this up about an hour,
getting cold and wet and sour
at her husband's lack of worry
for the tomcat. "He knows a trick or two,
tomcats always do.
He's no doubt crouched in George's woodpile—in some clever little cranny."
Well, my wife just kept it up,
and at the front door there was—yup—a shivering and supplicating tomcat.
So what had seemed a futile deed,
her getting cold and wet, indeed,
may have saved our tomcat from the blizzard.
Now the fire is lit, the tomcat's fed a bit,
and the cat and she are sleeping by the fire.
But of course I'm wide awake,
considering my mistake,

and marveling at her unstoppable
womanly concern.
There'll doubtless come a day
when that tomcat's put away;
I'll hear her cry and say
"I loved that tomcat."

Compunction

I can experience a tangle of emotion
concerning right and wrong
here in my warm and well-lit study
where a thousand distractions
urge me on.
So I'm fascinated, warm,
new ideas swarm,
take up my muse-infested brain.
But even then I squirm,
feel myself a guilty worm
conflated by ideas and distinctions;
concerns that hide from me
that pure morality,
that undefined compunction
by which a'Kempis would be torn.
God grant me some protection
from myself.

Exposure

Why this internal fuss?
I didn't steal anything
or murder anyone,
didn't point a loaded gun
at anyone but myself.
So why should I feel
Pepe's mortifying sting
as though I sat too near the king
and had been politely asked to move?
In just this very way
it pains me so to say
I was a boy, a weakling
with my feelings.
With no more to recommend me
than a stray dog, hungry, friendly,
I let my bleeding, inmost feelings
show; it was as though
I was an unselfconscious worshiper
in thrall, dumb-struck, contrite, adoring
in the presence of the Host;
as though I'd offered up my precious most,
my very soul
to this unearthly sovereign beauty.
She was engaging, kind,
blessed me from her table
with little crumbs, sometimes was able
to let go a bit of bread.
I so admire the Gary Coopers,

John Waynes and tall state troopers
who squint forth with their feelings
safely locked within a safe.
So my occasional reaction is to find some satisfaction
in castigating any weak, unmanly
supplicating feelings in myself.
It's always been much better
to let some well-filled sweater
approach me and recommend herself.
So I can play the sovereign,
throw some crumbs
and leave my feelings
undisturbed upon a shelf.
The only problem being
that it keeps me far from seeing
what I've never seen before
about myself:
that I am one of
many beggars at the gate.

A Man's Man

My junior year I took an unforgettable
18-hour overload: organic chemistry,
inorganic chemistry, engineering calculus,
genetics and Intermediate Russian;
I had an A in everything but Russian,
but by December I was overwhelmed.
One Friday evening, depressed and weeping,
I could only hope for Bs.
My father cancelled a Saturday appointment,
took the whole day off to spend with me.
at a hot springs he knew we got hour massages,
then steak dinners where there was a sawdust floor.
Back home, relaxing, he told me
lots of compromising stuff about himself,
stuff to make him seem more human in my eyes:
stealing from the dairy he worked for in school,
sleeping with my mother's best friend,
a parade of nurses, another doctor's wife who was hot for him,
a few special patients and, of course, telling lies of different sorts
to my mother Gracy, who would always sniff his shorts.
But best of all, when fourteen, like Zeus, he screwed a pig.
Did he get all muddy? I bet he did. I didn't ask.
What a therapeutic day. It made me feel much better
about those nights with Suzie Miller.
I got Bs except in calculus, where I still got an A,

and Russian, where I was glad to get a C.
Just couldn't get those declensions.
I still marvel at that pig.
I had to have a few more dates with Suzie Miller.

Perspective

I would be amazed if the 'universe' we can see turned out to be only a tenth of the universe we inhabit.

I would be amazed at how massive the actual universe is. If the actual universe turned out to be a hundred or a thousand times larger than the portion we inhabit, it would begin to surpass my ability to imagine. But what now appears to be the case is that the actual universe is 10^{23} (one hundred billion trillion) times larger than the portion of the universe we can see.

Our portion of the universe virtually disappears in comparison to the now inconceivably large universe of which we are a part.

Now consider an inevitable truth: there must be uncountable such universes scattered throughout the shapeless, eternal, infinite abyss that contains them. At the scale of this infinite abyss (if we may speak of such a thing), what to us are inconceivably large universes, are so infinitely small as not to exist. It is a gross exaggeration to say that, in comparison to the abyss, our monster universe, one of a numberless crowd of others, are something like dust particles at 30,000 feet.

Going through this exercise reminds me that I do not have the mental wherewithal to really grasp the situation I share with friends who already know what is necessary. I know just enough to see how ungraspable it is for me. But the little I know is like secret knowledge, especially knowing that anything, no matter how large, in comparison to the infinite abyss, is as nothing. Or from the standpoint of the abyss, the largest universe, and we with it, at that scale, really don't exist. Yet here we are, reading about how the Oxford English Dictionary was made. I am so glad I have been given this perspective. It gives me a needed bulwark against those who are more certain than I about what is important.

The Infinite Abyss

I believe I can begin to conceive
of a universe at least 10^{23} times larger
than our portion of it, the Hubble volume,
by scaling, making it a toy.
Doing this, the volume of the *actual* universe
in relation to ours might be conceived
as the Hubble volume in comparison
to half a cubic mile.
Even though a bit of a strain,
I can even begin to conceive
of some unnumbered non-number of these
monster universes, picturing them as
dust particles in a Dustbowl dust storm,
all spread out over Kansas.
But with the abyss itself,
even in the toy version of my thought,
I have a seemingly unsurmountable difficulty.
It is not, particularly, with its eternal existence,
after all, it is always there when I think of it,
a $10^{\wedge}$infinite perdurability, always there,
always has been, like the Rasmussens on Maple street.
What I don't get is the extentless extent
of the abyss, the fact that it can have no shape
and goes on forever in every direction,

the endless far away being the problem.
I want to get there but I can't,
no matter how far I go, it's always just as far.
I guess I have to try to be content
with where I am,
surrounded by something
I can't understand.

More About Myself

Am I prudent?
In a way I am,
in a way I'm not.
I flirt with girls I should not,
consid'ring the ripe wisdom of my age.
Because with due reflection
it's clear that my affection
is often smiled upon as harmless
to anyone but me.
If I think that I could dare
some winsome lady's bed to share
I'd be subject to a fright
that sometime in the night
I'd be prone to fall asleep
just when her passion beckons.
So I've been drumming on a tree stump
I thought a well-made drum.
Why I couldn't tell the difference
makes me think I'm dumb.
Maybe I am.
I'm just not quite conspicuously stupid.
I have this mystical insistence
that when I'm thrown a crumb,
a loaf of bread is wafting
its aroma and perchance
I've been offered some.
So I seize of this idea
that if I start to drum

on any stump I see
I might enchant the tree that's missing.
Is this gematria or some sum kabbalistic?
or just my tree-stump drum?

Vanessa

Yesterday, I bless the day,
I chanced to see Vanessa playing
Bach's best toccata on
her living violin.
Stirred by her conquering presence…
I knew, I saw a rhapsody,
this oriental beauty,
serene there at the ready,
violin in hand, already hypnotizing me
and maybe too, the solemn orchestra—her significance,
significance I share by watching her,
by floating on the air—her initiate perfection;
her fingers prancing on the strings
like a manic spider
in a courting dance,
that frenzied violin
outpacing Paganini.
And then the more amazing thing:
she'd lift her eyes up from the strings
and with a sleight of hand
that wasn't even there,
move through the quickest
dithyrambic passage of them all
spoofing the while
with a careless incandescent smile.
Earth's thoughts weren't there,
they'd passed away
as I watched this vision play,

shamelessly transfixed in adoration
a joy the heavenly host must know,
possibly God's holiest libation.
The orchestra was stiff and straight
surprised, undone to find her
so relaxed in her effusion,
Bach's Toccata in D Minor.
When Vanessa Mae began to hymn
that all-embracing thunder,
such a trance I'd never seen,
such lost emotion under
her flawless beaming face.
While I watched Vanessa
the world I knew was gone away,
afloat in spirit soaring
far above this earthly fray.
How such perfection can
be visited on man
confounds my reason,
stuns me into reverence.
I know I'm seeing Heaven's light,
hearing it aright for the first time,
keening for a splendor
never heard or seen before,
idolatry at heaven's door!
A loveliness, a music
I'd never known before,
an immortal goddess playing so,
standing alone upon the shore
of a galaxy unknown
with a supernatural ease
like a condor on the wind,
composure unbelievable,
a laughing smile just when
in a that middle presto
she plucks the strings

now and again.
I could yet breathe
and watch her.
Where Bach falls to lighthearted play
braiding themes that seem to say
now we're dancing on the clouds
with an airborne backing choir,
imagination finds its Waterloo.
The playful music changed her mood,
the orchestra then understood a little miracle:
that she'd actually been looking over
Bach's massive German shoulder
as he wrote those consecrated lines.
What now baffles me
are restless thoughts I seldom see—how insignificant I am,
how insignificant we are.
Does it matter she'll grow old,
that her confidence will fail,
confused and distressed
in stumbling error?
When she'll no longer be this bold,
and her precious hands I fear
will have a little tremble?
No. She can only be immortal.
So when I see some antique lady,
may I recall Vanessa Mae,
that what's divine is all still there,
a rhapsody of yesterday
in every counted hair.
With thin and palsied hands,
I'll know she's sending forth
her own divine rendition
of an unforgotten song.

Epiphany in a Forest

When I had accomplished
most of what I had to accomplish
in my work
and was about to retire,
I had a dream one night.
I was leading half a dozen
graduate students
on a walk down a gentle
wooded slope, looking for something,
I had no idea what.
Tired at noon, we ate our lunches,
and agreed on a short rest.
I found a grassy place beside a tree
and took a nap, a strange
sleep within my sleep.
Then I was awakened—a light touch on my shoulder.
I looked up, and
a timid, startled student said,
"I just wanted
to touch your greatness."
I awoke with tears
dripping on my pillow.
This dream must have been
what all that work was for.

Hobbs

Our cat Tom Hobbs
new indoor job's
to keep warm by the fire,
cavort and play
most of the day,
but sometimes to retire
to my dear lady's lap,
loud purring his proud lyre.
Then if Tom should jump away
with another cat to play,
even for a moment, say,
some catnip fine,
cats' semi-legal drug today,
will often bring him back,
this time to take a longer nap,
drugged and prob'ly dreaming
of some other horny cat
or maybe baby bird.
Anyway Tom's here to stay,
eating cat food, getting fat,
our welcome philo<u>soph</u>ic cat.

...-13

"...-13 and going down,
the snow squeaks
when it's this cold.
I'm going for a run," she said,
"squeaky snow and all,"
putting on her parka red,
stocking cap,
woolen gloves and all.
"Then I'm going
back to bed
and dream
of sweltering summer
and maybe early fall."
Nothing like an old man's strife
to have a young athletic wife.
While she's gone,
which won't take long,
I'll stay inside
and do some
exercising too.
I'll prob'ly do some pushups,
maybe one or two.
Don't want to overdo
just prior to an
Olympic nap,
something I can do
with great elan.

Riding into a Dust Storm

One summer dust storm,
I rode out past the dairy
to where it's dry-land wheat
or unfenced brown grass prairie.
Pumping like John Henry
hardly made me creep 'or consistently contrary
sliding sand beneath my feet
and little sharpened grains
that stung my face.
The wind was getting scary.
I'd ridden out to see
this monster rolling in,
the most exciting fun
I could imagine.
The western sky, a grey-black wall
with shades of dirty gold,
was quickly getting closer.
Were mother here 'twere pretty clear
she'd be sure to scold.
But I remember thinking then
that neither I nor any kid
should be questioned why or when
we do the things we do.
Sometimes a guy
just needs to watch a dust storm.
Back up Kansas Avenue,
shirttail raised up for a sail,
I went careening,

flying like a hero home,
propelled by winds too strong for that.
I did it anyway. It was so dark
some cars were parked,
unsure where they were at.
Luckily I knew the way
and didn't have to peddle.

Infinity Again

There would seem to be some parity,
no philosophic difference
between infinity
and the infinitely small.
But whereas we think
there is a lower brink
beneath which nothing
measurable can be,
namely the Planck-length,
10^{-33} centimeters;
there's no upper limit to infinity.
So the best that I can do
to scale infinity
is to set the longest distance we can see,
the distance to our universe's edge,
to the Planck length
and compare that to the universe's edge
or whatever longer distance
I'm able to imagine.
Then this extended distance
so unimaginably large
is set to the size of a sand grain
in a dust storm over Kansas,
all of which
will disappear in the abyss.

This may give me
a rough scale
by which to grapple
with how little I can see
of infinity,
which unlike my toy model
doesn't stop.

Monitor Off

With the monitor off,
in the dark with my headphones on,
to the unearthly strains
of the 7th symphony,
I keen my way across
this little galaxy,
riding on the strains,
the unearthly strains
of this unearthly symphony.
Endings were always hard for him,
but somehow I think the end for me will be easy.
I'll just turn the monitor off
and ride away
on the strains
of this unearthly melody.

Guilt

It's guilt that makes me worry,
causes me to hurry,
stumble on the mat,
skin my knuckles in the workshop,
makes me lose my hat.

Just the least infraction of halakhah that I know,
even an inaction,
or just being slow,
impugns the very spirit
wherewith up I chanced to grow.

What's needed for correction,
a bold friend said to me,
is deliberate election
of criminality.

That solution made me ponder
on one delicious sin
I tend to imagine
time and time again.

In my meditation
I turned this o'r and o'r;
decided that frustration,
relinquishment and more
was wiser far and better,
would get me safe ashore
and wouldn't trouble me with
skinned knuckles anymore.

On the Jersey Shore

There is a station story 'bout a New York fireman.
Casey was his name;
a big good-natured fellow,
a favorite of the men.
In a fire by the river,
two kids for help had cried.
he didn't wait for orders
but made his way inside;
used his safety blanket,
to carry them back out,
but thinking one was missing
ran back with a shout
"Hang on there, kid, we're coming…
Ya know we'll get ya out!"
When the fire was over…
where was Casey? Both children
now were sleeping in the truck.
"No man was ever better,"
someone said.
"Nah," declared the Chief…
"From that second story
he'd a dove into the river…
Bet he's now at Stacie's
on the Jersey shore
having ham and eggs for breakfast,

telling lies about the fire.
That intrepid rascal's
done things like that before."
"Yeah, yeah," chimed in the others,
"that's gotta be what happened.
He's on the Jersey shore having breakfast."

Raking Leaves

Once raking leaves in my front yard
I had a merry vision,
among the leaves a levitatious meditation on religion.
I'd be the pope, have lots of apostolic rope—inspiration started flaming from
the rake and from my yard!
I'd make infallible decisions, meritorious disquisitions,
benedictions to each and every sad and lonely female heart.
Repentant all-girl congregations in their tee shirts I'd baptize,
then we'd frolic and go swimming, rapt in sacrosanct exemption,
theophanic incandescent angels, nothing left to hide.
Then on a beach where we'd be lounging, my miter laid aside,
after they'd gone swimming, in glad salvation brimming,
they'd all seek more convocation with their pope, I might confide.
I'd bless them 'neath the sun with a loving papal stroke
and let them form a solemn line to kiss my finger—holy joke!

My leaves I then stopped raking,
sanguinary infusion of a papal reverie:
I had started wond'ring, could I improvise communion
and maintain my 'er inerrant papal dignity?
Yes! As the incarnate Cheering Spirit, I would deign to offer
Myself, my private Sacraments with due solemnity.
Such beatific fun! from which lesser popes might run,
I'd sanctify as High Church edict,
High Church theophany.
Having come to this conclusion,
having granted absolution
to His Holiness Himself,

to the newly virgin girls,
the leaves and trees,
I smiled my papal smile
and kept on raking.

Sir Thomas

I call him Thomas,
my wife calls him Hobbs,
our big Norwegian Forest cat,
Sir Thomas Hobbs.

We got him at a shelter
where he ruled the roost,
so placid when we left there,
we didn't have to boost him in the car.

He just took right over
much as if to say,
"Don't worry folks,
I'll get you home,
just watch, I'll show the way.

Still growing, getting rounder,
he'll be a thirty pounder.
He could keep a fox at bay
just by smiling.
You should see his paws,
they're big as silver dollars
not including claws.
They're surely for snowshoeing
on soft Norwegian snow.

After showing him affection once
I tried to walk away.
But he snagged my pants
with one big claw quite as if to say,
"Hey, Doodledoo, get back here,
I'm not quite through with you."

The Sought-For Understanding

If I approach a grasp of the greater reality,
glimpse the meaning of infinity and its creations;
if I can grasp what it means to be here,
infinitely small in the scheme of things;
if I can begin to grasp what by its nature
is impossible to grasp,
even if I can nod in that direction…

If my experimental concept of infinity, eternity,
breaks all bounds and must remain my secret,
what can this be like for me?
What response does this imbue?
I actually know. It is subsumed,
it means I stretch and yawn
like a jungle cat taking a few steps out of his lair,
startled by the color and variety before me
and know this is all for me.
This is the answer, imagine that!
Infinity is all for me—an axiom true for eternity.

Now maybe I can
get back to sleep.

Uncertainty

Reading recent
cosmology,
creates a fog
of uncertainty,
more or less
what an ant
might see
of proton decay,
of monster
black holes,
of integrating
Planck time
to eternity.
Should I not
be content
with what
I've been lent,
my ant-pile
sagacity?

House of the Dead

There are several books I've read
that help me with depression,
with the soul-sickening dread
that haunts me on occasion.

Fyodor's House of the Dead's
by far the best I'd say.
The lice that occupied his bed,
the dreary day by dreary day,
the monthly baths, the convict smell,
the roaches in the soup,
the leathery bread, the bread of hell,
the lack of any humor,
the floggings, shaving of the head,
the endless cold, the endless dread,
If there was hope, that hope had fled,
there wasn't any future.
Dostoevsky's little book
never fails to cheer me up.

That Last Hug

I saw your eyes, your moist blue eyes
at that last hug you gave me,
I felt your breath upon my neck,
I felt the love you didn't get
in that tiny moment.

How like the sweetest dream that was,
a dream I can't forget,
the unexpected feeling of
your breath upon my neck.

My Father's Eyes

They slanted down like Rommel's,
but they had more of a twinkle;
they said,
"You know that I think well of you—you ornery rascal."

Nothing was more captivating,
those eyes filled with confidence.
You believed all they were saying,
disbelief had not a chance.

They had a healing power,
they made the spirit dance.
they mesmerized the marrow,
no illness had a chance.

When I look into my own eyes
I can see my father there,
smiling at me deep inside.
It's then I know he's there.

How I've grown to love him.
If I could only share
the great good will, the humor
everybody saw was there
in my father's eyes.

Tree House Prayers

The summer I turned thirteen
I built a tree house in the tree
behind our house near the alley.
I built it with used lumber
I found molding on a rack,
I got a hammer, saw and level
from the storage shed in back.
Six 8-foot 2x4s, a box of nails, steel cleats and more
my dad supplied; he let me charge them
at the Hawley lumber store.
I built it like a bunker tucked up in the sky,
triangular with three-foot walls
a little roof, where, if it rained,
you could keep a few things dry.
I had a fine contraption to lift my dog up there
a canvas bag, a rope and pulley—didn't seem to scare her in the least.
A use ecclesiastical consecrated this construction.
I could sleep up there at night,
and, saying prayers to Sally White,
cogitate without fear of worldly interruption;
solemn syncopated prayers
with no worldly interruption.
When the tree house was all done,
my dad climbed up and told me "Son
what a splendid job you've done!
This thing by golly ought to win a prize!"
Now I'm 75, I for the first time realize
he never had a tree house as a kid;

the 2x4s and nails were his imaginary fun,
climbing up, telling his son
what a splendid job he'd done. What a splendid job
God did when he made my dad.
It makes me sad he never had a tree house.

The Dark

I'm not a captive of the dark
where I sip my coffee.
There's an existential spark
that lights the way.
I've come to love my darkened room,
the world I do not fear,
often my cheeks can glad assume
a warm and joyful tear
just about the morning, and
simply being here
with my cup of coffee.
I can float about the universe,
yet always know it's me.
I'll sometimes scratch an awkward verse
about a monster galaxy
or maybe a black hole
that gets me falling free
of ordinary time the closer that I get;
or even more about the music
that stirs me allegretto,
while I gravitate and let go
psychologically;
I know I'll soon become
the singularity a high school professor
sneered and nicknamed me.
In a way I am the universe,
the marvels that I see.
With the Almighty I converse,

For Him a hymn I might rehearse,
approved, confirmed and none the worse
for knowing it's just me
with my cup of coffee.

Dignity

That essential human dignity
that cannot be
violated with impunity,
I have violated
to my sorrow many times.

It stings my conscience
to the marrow
when I see that
my presumption,
uninvited,
plowed a furrow
where a furrow oughtn't be.

Where pride descries
a new dimension
wafting forth from
old established ties,
a heart now hot
from new contention,
caught in its
accustomed lies…

Nothing worse can be imposed
no castigation,
no straighter cut
by any scissor,
no more severe
laceration
falls on the back
of any prisoner.

More on My Father

Once in college,
sitting alone in the dark
I was for the briefest moment
overcome, made dizzy,
by a vision fragmented
as though in a kaleidoscope,
the fullest view yet of my
permanent immersion
in my father, his life,
my inseparable identity in him.
It dismayed me to be such a captive;
I knew the vision would pass, and it did.
Now, more than fifty years later,
more than forty years since his death,
I am revisited by an equal, this time
sustained immersion in these now
technicolor understandings.
They rack me with emotion,
cause me to exult, make me sad enough to weep
that it's been so long since I've seen this.
If I die now
I will carry a little bit of him with me.

Scolded

Do I have a program?
My friends all think I do.
But there seems doubt that I am
responsible and true.

From reproach I tend to smart,
a scolding makes me blue;
long continued I will part
and loneliness will do.

I'll look on trees admiringly,
how stolid there they stand,
more serene, complacently,
than I ever can.

What's there for me
when I'm upset?
A stationary tree, an example for me yet

that knows not how to travel.
Does it remember or forget
how winter storms unravel
its fittest branches yet?

Is it always thinking, yes,
of what can I be sure?
—Of winter storms and summer bliss
perhaps one season more?
Do trees believe in God?
I suppose they're sure
of roots that penetrate the sod,
telling the tree: yes, you'll endure.

I so marvel at a tree
that to reproach is blind
to whom affront is meaningless,
the worst the tree will only find amusing.

So I'll go back home again
and be more like a tree,
with thicker bark and cambium
in tune with all I see.

The Cello Player

When I think of composure
It's of her iridescent face
sitting straight up at her cello,
a picture perfect, perfect grace.

In the Brandenburg six,
that bumpity-bump cantata,
her face is the face
of a prayerful Madonna.

Her bow plies the strings,
her left fingers all do prance,
and her unmoving face
makes her seem as in a trance.

She isn't "pretty"
but so heavenly serene
that I know how a goddess
can constitute a dream.

I watch this performance
again and again
I never tire of seeing her,
admiring her again.

When I think of composure
I'll think of her face
showing me perfection,
showing perfect grace
there at her cello.

Faust in His Study

I'm not in trouble, mostly,
sitting in my study,
resolved not to invoke
any trouble anymore.

No matter how alluring
be the trouble that were stirring in
the trouble-hungry sinews
of my trouble-hungry soul.

I can call some wizened buddy
on my cell phone in my study,
confess how I've been shopping
for some trouble every day.

Tell him how I just can't help it,
how I keep my study lamp lit
composing philosophic nonsense,
shooing trouble thoughts away.

But my unconscious program
seems to indicate that I am—poor unlucky fella—
constituted that away.

I read a meditation book
that has me lying by a brook,
musing on some wispy homiletic
that whisks me far away.

Then I awake to winsome trouble
there, snuggling by my side
—the sort of winsome trouble
from which a fella cannot hide…

So now the meditation's through,
almost any winsome
nearly fatal heart attack would do
to buoy my bookish spirit.

Code Knocking
(Second-Handing Arden's Poem)

The most cold sweat producing
sound I've ever heard
didn't come from explosions,
or gunfire or shelling
that kept us all interred
in our foxholes.
'Twas a code we were sure
from the left loud and clear,
a ratta-tat business-like knocking.
On hollow bamboo,
the sound carried so true,
you knew it could be heard for a mile.

'Twas a sick'ning fright
when there came from the right
another answering tattoo,
talking jolly, it would seem,
now they had us in between
the left and right code-talkers
on their ratta-tat bamboo.
It bathed us in hysteria,
surrounded, outgunned,
they knew where we were
with no place to run.
In any situation now
where I can't see what to do

I sometimes hear the knocking
and know that Hell is stalking me,
because I hear the knocking of that
Viet Cong bamboo.

Acrobatics

If I can be patient,
If I can be kind,
If I can see time as my friend,
then I can be quiet,
peaceful and quiet,
have a dutiful, useful and beautiful mind.
If I can be grateful,
never be hateful, rather be
thoughtful and biding my time,
my conscience will bless me,
bliss will caress me;
perchance there will come
a moment sublime.
But then what the hell,
my good heart will swell,
I'll be doing so well,
I'll gallop away with a loud rebel yell,
leaping canyons, soaring aloft,
flying so high I'm a speck in the sky,
spurning virtue, my privilege,
spurning the cost.
Then I'll plummet down,
like a meteor down, leaving a fiery trail,
bereft of my crown,
locked up in an insane asylum.
Only there can be found,
with my feet on the ground,

a yearning for peace once again,
the peace I have found
when I'm patient and kind,
have a dutiful, useful and beautiful mind,
and planning on doing it over again.

Scaling Space, Scaling Time

Yes, our toy space is still infinite,
even as an imagined toy.
Throughout there is a uniform, "scattered"
let us say, "nearly" nonexistent dust,
but "scattered" (with no end of it)
like a dense, invisible fog
matching the void itself—a mere thought.
Each generation of this dust/mist
pulses in and out of existence
in less than Planck-length time.
(That is to say, the 10^{100}-year life
of a universe is in our toy eternity something less
than 10^{-33} seconds—indeterminably brief
in unutterably, perdurably patient eternity.)
And think of this, with no beginning!
But the scale of space is quite as interesting:
space is forever in both extent and time,
no beginning, no end to either.
Universes and unimaginably large clusters of universes
are infinite in "number," where "number" is a joke;
all like the faintest mist throughout,
the toy yet infinite extent in which all that is must swim.
This mist of universes comes into existence and disappears
in a disappearing interval of "time,"

where like "number" "time" is a joke.
The infinitely small is the only possibility
at the scale of infinity,
the infinitely brief the only possibility
at the scale of eternity.

Moxie

What strikes me as pathetic 'bout the off'rings of my mind
is the godlike moxie
unquestioned as the rind
of an Osage orange smug beneath its tree,
or the carapace so thick
of a tough unsquashable
diligent wood tick
buried without having raised
the least alarm
in a sweaty unanesthetized
hard-working underarm.

It's so easy to forget
that scholars like Ben Zion
always have their lights on
always fear they may forget
some important reference.

But I exude my proclamations and
opinions quite as free
as the Oronoco cataract
or a dripping maple tree.

And if some wond'rous critic
were to stupidly invoke
any tiny quibble 'bout a verse 'twould be a joke.
So I rummage through my learning, think it vast as it can be.
If I didn't think this, could I even breathe?

1960s

There's something unnatural about life,
it's an engine demonic running on strife,
unable to slow down, unable to stay
thoughtful and quiet, unable to pray,
even rev'rently humming a song.

The country's addicted, racing along,
addicted to progress, change and invention,
obsessed with finding ten ways to perfection,
bigger and better, far faster of course.
All philosophers know that it's worse

—this need for winning, if always perverse.
this faster and faster, this mustn't slow down
on the way to the graveyard and into the ground.
Give me a break! I'll just wander around
with my backpack.

Beethoven's Face

I understand something about Beethoven's face
because I saw it as a kid,
its exact likeness on my friend John Beckwith.
John had the same unplumbed,
serious, pensive sincerity,
the same natural naivete,
the same capacity to understand
what he was looking at.
I can't see that famous painting of Beethoven's face
without seeing my friend John Beckwith.
When I took that mental snapshot,
he was studying how
to rebuild the hull of a derelict racing boat.
So sixty years later I see
I've been acquainted
with Beethoven since I was a kid.

Beethoven and Me

As a kid Beethoven was a klutz.
So was I.
He stayed that way and got worse.
So did I.
Somehow his drinking father set him up, in a good way and a bad.
So did mine. I ended up drinking, he didn't.
We both lived in contempt of everyone, he with justification, not I.
He couldn't speak or use language well.
I couldn't control my mouth, later dabbled in philology.
He had no use for Kant, Goethe, maybe never heard of Spinoza,
I worshiped them.
He was too brilliant and unique to be teachable.
I faked it.
Even as a kid he started soaring.
I sniffed gas, read Schweitzer and tried to pole vault.
He was honest and usually moral.
I was usually honest.
He became one with God.
I only know God through a wormhole.
He still goes to the end of the universe with the 7th Symphony.
I just watch with my little soul,
amazed.

Maimonides

I've studied most of Maimonides in translation.
Two places in Volume 7 of the Mishnah Torah
I laughed 'til I split
knowing he intended me to do so.
One place was about sleeping with your sister by mistake.
Once in the *Eight Chapters* I went into convulsions
over the shabbiness of my life.
Thanks to Yellin, Abraham and Strauss
I am beginning to think I know Maimonides,
But I should probably read the *Guide* a few more times.
I liked his candor in the Mishnah Torah
where he recommends:
"Pee when you must,
but only after three drips
When you're praying."

Prostitutes

Prostitutes, prostitutes, prostitutes all
Most women are like that, pretending to fall
for the man not his money, telling them all,
"Come and expand me, come make me scream
while I'm writhing beneath you caught up in a dream."

But the truth's a bit diff'rent a wise man told me.
The woman's the master 'er false for the fool
who'd part with his money, part with her fee,
part with the dignified man he would be.

Her pleasure's his money, his helplessness too,
an actress's pleasure in scripting the screw.

A man is by nature a dunce for a girl,
a brainless thing captured, no longer free,
snapped to a magnet like filings that swirl
on the paper of destiny held by a girl.

Is there any chance a good man can stay free?
…Free as a vacuum, free as a gap,
free to be wretched, alone, incomplete
'til safe once again 'tween a prostitute's feet.

Growing Old

Growing old, no longer bold, undetermined what will be.
Will the corruption, interruption that is coming certainly
inundate me, pound and drown me like a freezing winter rain?
Will a dim translucent curtain indemnify my dod'dring brain?
Will the sweet attending nurses sweetly mollycoddle me,
tell old friends that I'll get better if they chance to visit me?
Will the dirge, the ripe confusion render me a tattered rag?
Will frequent falls, frequent contusions cause me finally to sag,
justify their dire conclusion: "In your wheelchair you must stay."
Sagging, drooling, often weeping, often sleeping through the day.
But in that distant dismal day I know I'll carrion some way.
I'd better ride that motorcycle while I can.

Manhandled

The tale I tell is sad.
Did I deserve the little lad,
the friendly, playful boy,
the only kid his mother had
when she became my toy?
I only rarely played with him,
just when it was convenient.
Of all things less provident
I put off adopting him.

He was such a sensitive kid,
his drowned goldfish caused him to keen,
which makes much worse the thing I did
when he had turned thirteen.
Two or three small pigs I'd bought,
fenced them in a grassy spot,
found a handy bucket then
to give the pigs their water in—a stupid choice I'd soon regret.
Then the boy did I impound
each day to fill the bucket.
And coming home one day I found
the water low: and in the too-big bucket
an upended pig had drowned.

I scolded him unmercifully,
scolded him for *my* mistake,
cruelly, psychologically.
Only now I think I've found
I'd disinterred a trauma—the pet goldfish he thought he'd drowned.

He then ran away from home,
hitchhiked all the way and tried
to find where his real father died,
seeking an identity
he couldn't find with Lynne and me.
We later learned he'd changed his name
to his real father's—to my shame
a better dad than me.

We seldom then saw him again.
He'd lost his simple boyhood,
often found himself in trouble,
became a drinking, pot-smoking rebel.
He worked odd jobs here and there,
evading john law everywhere.
But since he was a Cherokee, at least a sixteenth part,
he lived on reservations, tried to make a lawful start.
For years in south Montana, he lived the cowboy life,
drinking, carousing, sometimes marrying a wife.

Left with a cherished daughter by a schizophrenic wife,
he changed his act and settled down, straightened up his life.
This daughter he then cared for in all his cowboy strife—a resurrected goldfish,
the first love of his life.
That's all I'd heard about his roaming,
Except as rumors have it, how the girl's devoted to him.
Lately I've heard he's sober, leads an honest life,
taken a friend, a rare delight named Willow for his wife,
He called and sounded happy. I was glad he did.
For once he didn't hesitate to tell us where he lived.

Now I'll recount what launched this thing: a forgettable debouch.
My wife's a redoubtable scrapper, I have a criminal mouth.
In a cataclysmic marital symphony, my own composition,
my stolid wife called the cops on me, showed not the least contrition.
These nice guys just advised me less intense to be,

behave myself, expostulate a bit more reasonably.
They also then approved a plan for me to pack a bag
and be gone a day or three, suggesting I not lag,
which is what I dutifully, disconcertedly did.

My prowess fallen to zero just then,
my stepson I thought I might drive up to see
in northern Wyoming, a long-deferred plan.
'Twas an 'er so long stomach-ache journey for me.
When I called, he invited my visit enthused, his reaction a comfort to me.

In Greybull he said he'd come meet me, show me the way to his "shack",
rolled up in a beat-up old pickup, a big lop-eared dog in the back.
With an oversized Nietzsche-like moustache,
a broken-down straw cowboy hat,
this lean lanky cowboy walked over to me. I offered my hand,
he smiled and said "No", gave me a bear-hug and wouldn't let go.
I crumpled inside, what a wretch I had been:
forty years absent, a stranger to him.
When at his wilderness cabin we sat, I unburdened to him
what a harsh and unloving stepfather I'd been. Both of us cried,
one man openly—in front of his dog, little daughter and wife,
overwhelmed, he so touched me—first time in my life.

I'm changed from the man I'm accustomed to be
—a stoical unemotional tree—
when he said, such a wonder, he'd forgiven me.
It pierced me inside, I could finally see: my little stepson
was better than me.
And wonder of wonders! This cowboy then called me his dad.

This day was amazing as sunshine in hell.
All the way home I cried like a baby. I'm crying still.
Could it be maybe my Heavenly Father's just manhandled me?
Yes, I believe that he has.

A Go-Ahead Gopher

I'm a go-ahead gopher
I never turn back;
I call it a virtue
to join my old track.

I always dig forward,
sing Riggidy Dig,
I never dig backward,
it's forward I dig.

I'm the happiest gopher,
by diggity dig. My credo is forward,
I don't care a fig for direction,
but if near the surface
it's downward I dig.
Close navigation is useless down here.

I never look forward,
I never look back,
I never question
the lay of my track.
Plumb-bobs and transits are useless down here,
just the clutter of ratiocination.

Who needs to look forward
or plan where to go?
Just watch out behind me
for dirt that I throw.

Polite conversation is useless down here.
I'm a powerful digger,
I seldom need rest.

I can munch on a grub
not even bereft of the munchiest,
crunchiest dirt on his chest.
Strict sanitation is useless down here.

To dig's my religion,
devoutly I dig.
Digging's my passion,
I'll dig 'til I die,
or maybe while digging get raptured.
But theology's perfectly useless down here.

When digging I know that
there's nothing to fear
from the Father, the Son, or the
so Holy Gopher, the mystical seer.
Confirmation is useless down here.

'Cause I dream of the stars,
imagine the music of Spanish guitars,
I've got the whole cosmos,
the universe here,
snug in my riggadig burrow.

Silence

Silence, the tool of sorcerers,
the engine of cognition, the familiar voice of God,
bellwether invention of genius, Moses' caduceus rod,
victorious over aggression, victorious over the flood.
It masters the muse of the keenest mind,
an answer to everything hurtful or kind,
a friend to the helpless, the bold and the meek,
sword of the powerful, sword of the weak,
the wizard's prescription for meaningless talk,
perdurable matrix of prayer and of love,
perfection of poetry, so far above
mere inspired thoughts that come to the mind;
the voice of an orchid, the voice of a tree,
the voice of the grass, moon and stars.
Talk is the lesson that's instructing me
in the durable durance of silence.

Kindness

Every person I see is a moment away
from abandonment, hopelessness, stark desolation
—this awful potential for hopelessness.
The least I can do is try to allay
this beloved brother's defeat with a smile
as we pass on our perilous way.
a pat on the back will often beguile
the sting of misfortune if just for a while.
The smallest emolument of a kind word
can keep the world turning, better the day.
Life's too short not to offer a smile.

Transference Love

Freud's essay on transference-love
indexed in volume 24
is 'er my loosely fitting glove,
though I don't always follow it
when 5th-stepping a neurosis.
A rule I often break
is with respect to candor:
private stories I relate,
similar stories to oblate,
transference to establish.
The rule I mustn't ever break
is falling for some lovely dish
and of her warmth advantage take;
derailing useful work and which
could land me in embarrassment,
if not a heap of trouble.
Yes, I'm a part-time analyst
enjoying pleasure double,
a 12-step psychoanalyst
consulting Freud if in a muddle.
My object's my sobriety,
another year, another chip,
a conscience clean, a conscience free,
protection from a fatal slip.
So there, my friend, there'll always be
discretion that is natural,
yet love-transference, hopefully,
that lands no one in trouble.

Our sharing last was wondrous fun:
I feel we matched each other's mold.
I wouldn't trade such tangling fun
for diamonds, jewels, or heaps of gold.
So please consent my friend to be,
we could be loving friends that see
each other's best, such friends as see
perfection in a friend.

A Morning Prayer

Keep me sober, sane and safe today, reasonably happy,
restrained yet confident to smile, grateful for sobriety,
hoping for some fellow drunk I can show the way;
if he's a real knee-walking drunk, inside he's just like me.

Give me a need to understand, not be understood,
sure of the peril of my path, remembering to pray,
grateful for the meetings, hugs, laughter, sense of love,
thankful to the One above for one more sober day.

Grocery Shoppin

I often offer so compliantly
to do the grocery shoppins,
and in the store can't help but see
those long bare legs and oscillating bottoms.

While in the produce section
it seems to me I oughta
ask some helpful lady to squeeze my avocada.

I feel an inspiration, I can't help myself,
to ask a tallish maiden
to reach some sorely needed item on an upper shelf.
If it's too high, I could offer then to boost her,
even if some matron said,
"What's this, a hen and rooster?"
With my groceries I start home,
driving with extra caution,
careful to slow for long bare legs
and oscillating bottoms.

To wife I'll say, "OH! what a day! But
for you I'll do it often.
If you'll just put this stuff away
I'll rest..." and think of long bare legs
and oscillating bottoms.

Cautions

Unintended I imagine things that keep me out of trouble,
like crashing with my motorcycle when I'm riding double
or chancing to be kissing Sue just when my wife arrives,
or slipping on some icy chute down a mountainside;
but one that leaves me filled with fear, extra horrified,
is where I've free-climbed far too far
up a vertical redoubt on some mountainside
and realize I've climbed too far, unable to proceed, unable to get back.
I suspect this is a metaphor for some un-thought-out tack,
some fine ambitious project far too big for me,
a metaphor that goes to show the plan's stupidity.

These brief imaginings I almost never mind,
except the one about the cliff where too far up I've climbed,
for they instruct me in a second something I should know:
not to be impulsive or do things just for show,
to consider what my options are, maybe not to climb too far,
returning safely to my car and driving slowly home.

Beethoven's Loneliness

Think of Beethoven's loneliness: it lasted all his life,
almost deaf at the seventh, stone-deaf at the incomprehensible ninth.
How can a man so alone in the world have so majestic a spirit
to send forth a music incomparably bold? I levitate listening to it.

Think of the silence that reigned in his room
while he penned those incredible lines.
Think of the loneliness turned into gold,
the heart's blood he left for mankind.

He knew by the 3rd he was to be deaf, but despite that a hero would be,
overmatching Napoleon 'fore he was dead, a far greater hero than he.
The seventh a rescue for others bereft of a way out of silence,
a way out of self,
that a way, an enlivening freedom is left for those in thought prisons like me.

Grandaddy Broadbrooks

In 1943, from up Mulberry street
Grandaddy Broadbrooks would walk down
shouldering his scythe.
A kid had heroes then of course,
but he was extra neat.
he'd cut the weeds in Grandma's yard,
was expert with his scythe.

When he was hot, he'd doff his shirt,
and show his sweating muscles lithe.
He told me he was 94.
I told him I was five.
He was a tall impressive man,
looked like a college kid,
I was fascinated by most everything he did.
Now and then he'd hone his scythe… kept it razor sharp,
he showed me how to do it too… 'twould whizz the hair right off his arm.
He said he'd learned to hone a scythe on his grandfather's farm.
He told me lots of scary tales 'bout farming history!

He'd be glistening with sweat, looking tan and tall. He'd say,
I have to visit Grandma's house, I have to take a pee.
Grandma was a widow then, seventy or more.
Of course I didn't realize this visit was his fee.
While he was gone, I'd guard his scythe, and whet the edge some more,
wond'ring why it took so long for him to take a pee.

Then he'd come back with Grandma's stew in a Mason jar,
tip the scythe up with his foot, catch it skillfully,
Even then I figured he was showing off for me.

Then Grandaddy Broadbrooks said:
"When these weeds have grown again,
you'll have grown some too, my friend".
I remember once he winked and said,
"Next time we'll talk again for sure."
I knew he was just how I'd be when I'm 94.

Alluvium

Whenever west I need to fare, the Basin-Range I travel.
All the beauty there to see, the brown grass and the loess;
the thing that fascinates me most is the alluvial gravel,
so uniformly sloping toward the valley floor.
The standard story: water-borne erosion is all that's needed for
explaining all these gentle slopes; so speculate no more.
I've heard this textbook palaver, unconscionably dumb.
If this were so there'd be creek beds in the alluvium;
but they're smoother than a baby's butt, a jello-mold-like breast.
It can't be rain that shaped them so, I put that thought to rest.
The answer's told, it seems to me, by their perfect symmetry.
What made debris so thus to creep? Microseismic activity!
All that's needed is a glance at Richter's jagged tracing,
The crustal jiggle we can't feel must keep that gravel shaking,
if even at the smallest scale 'twould cause it to be moving.
But geologists with self-respect still say it's just the rain.
This geologic prejudice has taught me to refrain
from proposing to geologists or trying to explain
what causes the alluvium to slope down to the plain.
I look and smile and think I know what seems so clear to me:
it's that subtle crustal jiggle, seismic activity
smoothing out the wrinkles of a rough topography.
That alluvium is beautiful to precious few but me.
After all, I'm like alluvium, to all appearance still,
but moving imperceptibly, sliding down the hill;
the rate of sliding slows with time, stirred by vibration fine
Eventually I'll come to rest, I'll be forever still;
but this morning I feel grateful for my microseismic life.

226

Motorcycle Prayer

Father,
Thank you for the moxie you passed on to me,
Thank you for Grandfather's balls, for Manx heredity,
thank you for the blood you spilled to keep our country free,
for being always present when the spirit beckons me;
for the graves at Ballabeg, alcoholics all;
for the long Norwegian arms
perfect for sword swinging,
for the absence of alarm, for
solitary singing—as I ride along,
For the tears, for vanished fears,

Thank you, Dad, that I am not
the drunken sot of times gone by,
for friends who say they love me,
for the checkered tarnished years
I now consider lovely;
for my crazy Uncle Caesar who lost two family farms
horsing 'round in Douglas town drinking, playing cards.
Thank you for the moxie you passed on to me,
Thank you for Grandfather's balls, for Manx heredity.
thank you for rhyming petards, creative versifying,
thank you for the manliness
you had when you were dying.
Thank you, Dad, for all I am, for 'er with me abiding,
Thank you, Dad, for being here,
especially when I'm riding.

Pushkin

Pushkin said he thought in rhyme,
the tsar thought him inverse,
scribbling out disloyal lines
in crass Cyrillic, Worse!

He could write a line so nasty'twould embarrass even me.
He'd sometimes ridicule the tsar
and still collect his fee.

True, few can rank with Pushkin—maybe Goethe or Shakespeare—
but I'm stuck with Arndt's translation,
my Russian's bad I fear.

The salient problem with his verse
(if I can be so free)
is horrible, interminable prolixity,
though always terse and meaningful
he goes on endlessly.

It's often oh so trivial too!
What's found there to repeat?
Perhaps he rates the ballyhoo,
but considered judgement says
we simple folks, less erudite,
are not beneath his feet.

Perhaps immortal Pushkin's
too great to denigrate.
I may read his works again,
but only after Felix Krull
and only when it's late.

Do I display my shallowness,
my private thoughts to voice?
but stuffing thought is hardly just—to swim upstream's my choice.

It could be an imperfection
in the way I view his art,
but I've not found a line in Pushkin
that stirs me, moves my heart.

Even Fyodor in prison,
when sick and with a choice
would rather sneer at Turgenev
than nod to Pushkin's voice.

But one immortal line I'll keep,
a line no one should mangle,
so good it almost makes me weep—that angels deign to tangle,
and where the girl can't help but arch
beneath the fond Archangel
in the Gabrieliad.

A Meeting

Sitting 'round the table,
they no longer drink.
Impossible! A miracle!
All have ceased to drink!
Coming in they greet me,
offer me a seat.
I feel such love for everyone,
they're just like me…
my heart… my eyes are wet.
I listen to the stories, former wretches I've just met,
I tell my own, it's just as bad, some think it's even worse,
a tale of true insanity, my last 'yet'—an unaccompanied hearse,
of everlasting dry vomiting, still a bad nightmare for me,
megalomaniac delusions, "You must not know who I am!",
of police, of strait jacketing, jail time, psyche wards three.
Tell how I sober, gained (I blush), some microhumility.
The more gruesome the story, the more they laugh and smile
for it illuminates the thoughts we share this little while.
Afterward we sit outside, maybe three or four,
regale the newest man with a few really shameful stories more,
convincing him he not a world-class drunk, not famous anymore,
but now fallen in with former drunks who know the drinking score,
professionals, not amateurs. Then they share again
just how they got right, how they finally found
a new Companion, who sustains, forgives, encourages, can understand.
"If you need it and you want it, you can be happy as these men.
But from what you've already told us, I think you might fit in."

230

The Elm

I measure my days
by my little Elm tree;
its trunk and its branches
are special to me,
so slender and eagerly
skyward they reach.
My kindness toward it
when I let it grow
would seem a reward
it is now giving me,
as though the tree loves me,
is that possible?
It moves me to see it there
standing so still
or in a breeze waving
its branches to me.
So strange the deep feeling
I have for that tree.

African Beauty

My parents had a carving,
their one true work of art,
an exquisite lady, starving,
her slender neck so gently arched,
high cheekbones, a subtle smile, perfect lips relaxed,
a face that surely must depict
something rather pleasant lying on her back.
But the point of this description
was the gently convex nose.
A perfect feature, I suppose—
that gave her such a regal face
One day she fell down from the place
she hung upon the wall.
Still a diapered toddler,
Mother said I bit her nose,
(something I don't recall).
Mother gave scant notice to this lady on the wall.
The fact her boy had bit her left new teeth marks on her nose,
captured then her fancy, became a favorite tale she'd tell
when the chance arose.
When I was twelve, my sister nine—there seemed to be no reason—
she also bit this famous nose
and on my fame encroached.
But this carving now is precious,
hangs on my study wall.

The important thing about that face, withal,
are my sister's teeth marks
on that nose, reminding me:
imitation is a priceless form of flattery.

My Daughter

Driving home down Santa Fe,
my first wife scolded me,
stoplight after stoplight,
kept scolding me real bad.

When she'd finally finished with her wrath,
my daughter, nine-years old
from the back seat smiled and said
"I think you're perfect, Dad."

Sundays

Sunday mornings, my wife away at Church,
I've begun to listen to Vivaldi's cello concertos,
or, for a special treat, Beethoven's seventh symphony.

Listening I am with God in his lonely perfection.
Can I not keen to be with Him? Can I not weep?
This is my Church, my Synagogue,
Amidah, Hymn of Glory.

No Address

According to Alan Guth's inflation theory (that first made sense of Big Bang expansion) the universe of which we are a part is 100,000 billion billion times larger than the universe we can see, the same as the volume of the earth compared to that of a volley ball. According to the Copernican Principle even the actual far larger universe cannot be unique, nor can celestial units of any size be unique. So the idea of numberless universes—an idea with which many cosmologists are still struggling—is conceptually inevitable.

Surely this is true. Our unsuspectedly large universe is—let us say—only one of a large accretion of similar universes, each accretion resembling a spiral galaxy. Each galaxy-like accretion would then (perhaps) consist of one hundred billion universes—much like galaxies in our Hubble volume. Let us call this giant spiral accretion of universes an urgalaxy. And we might remember: there are at least one hundred billion galaxies beside our own here in our volley ball sized universe. Like all such gravitational accretions, the multiverse urgalaxy would be rotating—but imperceptibly because of its size: it might have, e.g., an angular velocity of one Planck-length per 10^{100} years. At this rate of spin, every universe in the accretion would wink in and out of existence before any point on the urgalactic circumference could even be detected to move with respect to its neighboring multiverse urgalaxies. Just as there are galactic clusters in our volley ball sized universe, there may be clusters of spiral multiverse urgalaxies rotating even more slowly.

This being true, something of an ultimate vision is available. If space is infinite and eternal (it has to be), then one spiral multiverse urgalactic cluster must be but one of an infinity of such clusters in infinite space. So where are we? Since there is no shape or edge that may be assigned to it, nor any fixed point in infinity, location is not a valid concept. So we needn't speak of homelessness, we know we orbit 'round our star. It's just that we have no address and don't know where we are.

Chagrin

Chagrin, chagrin,
looks something like a grin
a grin contorted by remorse
and silent facial mocking,
unintended and spontaneous of course.
It substitutes for verbal sparring,
exiting, absconding,
takes but a moment and then goes away.
It always happens when alone,
too obvious, expressive for display.
This solidified dishonesty,
the sound of capture every day
seems a prompt, a que for me
to grit my teeth and pray.
I suppose it puts chagrin lines
on my face.

Planetology

What I am given to understand so far about recent planetology is as follows. First, I take it, the mass of a star can be calculated by its luminosity and red shift, the speed and distance at which it is receding from us. The mass of an exoplanet (how this is distinguished from the cumulative mass other exoplanets I do not know)—and this is new—can evidently be determined from small, pulse-like deviations in the star's recession. When the exoplanet in its orbit swings toward us, the star's recession increases in speed slightly, when it swings away from us, it causes the star to slow slightly, causing a pulse in the star's red shift. This pulse, the distance of the exoplanet's orbit from the star, and the star's mass permit calculation of the exoplanet's mass.

More exciting, we can now apparently tell whether photosynthesis is—or has been—taking place on certain exoplanets. The principle is that individual atmospheric gases (oxygen being of particular interest) absorb light of a characteristic frequency. If, say, there is significant oxygen in an exoplanet's atmosphere (and the planet's orbit crosses in front of the star), for the brief time the exoplanet is illuminated by the star as it dips behind it, there will be a deficit in the exoplanet's light at the frequency of oxygen absorption/emission—indicating the presence of oxygen in the planet's atmosphere. If photosynthesis alone can account for atmospheric oxygen (this is true as far as we know), that planet can be assumed to have been supporting life for some time.

How's this for new information? Wow! This is all new to me. And of course it indicates an incredible increase in technology and technique. As I understand it, this has mainly worked with large planets, but it is increasingly being applied to smaller earth-like planets. Enormous numbers of life-supporting planets may be found yet in our lifetime.

The Flat Earth

To learn I'm on a turning globe—I thought the earth was flat—
upsets a fine stability:
I don't know where I'm at.
And then… the sun is just a star
like millions we can see,
I start to think, "Is Mother real?
What about this dirt I feel?
Have I been tricked, or can I still
believe it's really me?
Is this why I'm haunted now
by this uncertainty?
If I could know the earth is flat
and not a turning globe,
knowing itself's a suspect art,
a crazy-maker blown apart.
So do I now just play the part
of some uncertain Hamlet?"
"This skull I hold was once so bold
knowing the earth was flat,
it's left behind uncertainty,
with confidence is growing old
and knows the earth is flat.

Etiology

I was born, I didn't plan it.
Didn't even pick the planet,
didn't pick the galaxy,
wasn't even sure 'twas me,
didn't have a known address
until I found my mother's breast.
Here I found my occupation—turgid nipple's my obsession,
those breasts the universe to me,
gave me milk, enchanted me.
Embedded was an apogee,
the best of heaven offered me,
I soared aloft, from earth set free,
just me and mother's nipple.
My bone marrow later knew
it only took a drink or two
to recapture mother's breast,
find sweet oblivion, ever best,
happy not knowing who I am,
happy dreaming once again,
a nursing alcoholic.

Listening

I sometimes listen with my eyes
observe folks with my ears.
talking heads I don't despise,
heads that broadcast joys and fears.

So many things need not be said
I'm finding, listening, knowing,
I've learned to listen unafraid…
unafraid my thoughts are showing.

I find a beauteous symmetry
in quick returning smiles
that say you're you, that say I'm me, I love you in a smile.

Collar Marks

An old horse, I heard my grand-dad say,
that's long been used for plowing,
has neck marks that never go away
smooth hairless places showing
where the harness pressed
each day he'd pull and keep the furrow turning.
A horse can't see the collar marks
there on his aging neck,
but they speak of honest work,
where the harness pressed.
Were I such a horse I'd say
if I have collar marks today
they're where the harness used to be.
They make my owner proud of me.

My Quantum Faucet (A Ziegler Madrigal)

Sitting in my favorite chair looking at the sunrise
it seems incredible to me to know the earth is turning,
to know about our orbit 'round the sun,
to know about our spiral galaxy,
to know a hundred million galaxies have spun
for fourteen billion years
in the Hubble volume we can see—our universe the smallest part.
To be pretty sure there are
within the infinite panoply of universes
among their unnumbered stars
infinite copies of me and you,
of everything there is,
each cluster of universes like a dust grain
in an endless dust storm,
dust storms in themselves that must make evanescent clusters
lost in any number in a forever with no end, no start.
The latest quantum math predicts others just like me
looking out their window at a sunrise,
each knowing others are thinking thoughts like 'me',
wond'ring what he'll read this week to others copied faithfully,
exact copies of Chuck, Kathleen, Arden, Carleen, Phil and Verity
and Sandra who always gets there late.
Another thought is lurking, quantum math predicts
each of us will soon be born in the order which
every event in all our lives repeats itself somewhere.
Every thought, every sunrise seen here from my chair
has happened and will happen forever everywhere.
Many Beethovens will be born and live eternally,

infinity has always rung, will always hum
the seventh symphony.
So it is that I've been sitting looking out my window,
time without beginning, without end,
planning to fix that dripping faucet
that has always been
and always will be dripping.
Even if I fix it.

The Perfect Rock

Often when I take a walk
I'm looking for the perfect rock,
one that's smooth, will fit my hand,
has one flat side, is rounded and
pretty much symmetrical.

A rock like this of perfect size
I now consider quite a prize.
I toss it some to check its weight
and if it's right can hardly wait
to take it home and wash it.

When it's dry, I'll cut some cloth,
enclose the rock and snip some off
leaving half an inch for border
so the edges can turn under
while I sew it up.

With its perfectly closed suture
my little monolith is clad,
maybe just the picture of
how other rocks would like to be:
in modest dress the model of now well-dressed domesticity.
I imagine they're much happier.

Graceful Aging

I'm out of bed,
the coffee's made,
the cats are fed,
and all my pills are taken.
I find my chair,
the room is dark,
It's quiet there
looking out my window.
Methodically
the sun will rise
and set unstoppably.
It's no surprise
my trees and grass are growing.
I couldn't pay
or be more blessed
for one more day,
looking out my window.
My mind is dull,
the thoughts I mull
are full of imperfection.
My grass I'll mow,
and slowly plod,
but still I go
and thank God I'm still breathing.

I know I'm old,
decrepit, slow;
but I'm still bold
on my motorcycle.
Sometimes I pass a speeding semi—Yeah-hoo!
So much for graceful aging.

The 6th Symphony

In the second movement of the 6th symphony
a strong glad heart is weeping,
an eagle that accepts a broken wing,
a glad heart is weeping beneath a stolid face,
a sadness hidden by the sheerest lace

a soul more than beautiful is weeping,
from an aching lonely soul is squeezing
such a lilting melody divine.

If the Almighty's voice were heard 'twould be no different from
this encrypted metaphor.
God would sing or maybe hum,
and hold Beethoven in his arms.
He'd hum this very symphony.

A Flea

Does a flea think to itself
"I have one life to live?
What of a one-day mayfly,
a two-day katydid?"
Or does he think his tiny soul
in other fleas will hide?
Can he remember being there
the night that Issa died?
Issa didn't swat him
but chose to let him be
and wrote a poem, his last one.
a poem to a flea. It went:

The night is long for you fleas too,
and lonesome just like me.

Kobayashi Issa was
the greatest of Haiku poets.
The translation I remember goes:
For you fleas too,
the night must be long,
it must be lonely.

My Leaning Elm

The first eight feet of my Elm tree is leaning toward the north.
The natural solution were to prop it.
But with all my disapproving, I've not noticed it before,
the middle part's already curved about,
the top part's growing straight and out, a little toward the south.
It looks as if the tree knows what it's doing.

Thus sinuously grows the tree;
the problem was I couldn't see what the tree was doing.
It was dancing from the start, a youthful undulation,
each growing, graceful, leaning part,
moving to some glad impulse, I think it hears a melody.
I didn't understand my tree, the slowness of its treeful grace,
its insipient, so graceful sinuosity, a secretly inspired ingenuity.
I have a joyful, dancing tree.
My lack of understanding makes me sad!

A Hermit

When Tao Yuan Ming was old, he said
something like this:
To keep the measure until I'm dead
would mean unendurable hardship.
I'll be a hermit, I'll live in a shack,
plant a small garden, never look back.
Who knows, I might write a marvelous poem,
sipping my wine—there'll be "no one at home".
A vegetable garden in back I will grow,
I'll live on the vegetables that I will grow.
I'll always be happy, never be sad,
remembering often the joys that I've had.
On books I'll be carried, flying away
off in the universe. I know I'll stay
enraptured while hoeing my garden.

Retrospect

All my life I've lived by impulse,
haven't needed hesitation;
mistakes aplenty the result,
a checkered life it's always been.

I never waited for the time,
or for the just-right situation,
when all the ducks were in a line:
I'd curse the ducks and move on.

But now I'm getting old and slow,
I bless the times I have to wait,
I've learned to relish going slow,
it's my good luck to hesitate.

I bless the peace I've never had,
for sometimes knowing wrong from right,
for sometimes knowing good from bad,
for understanding as I might
how much better in my sight
to be at ease and sleep at night.

Poesy

I have a sage companion who lives inside of me,
who knows that prose is always best, despises poetry;
he thinks if rhyme were given rest 'twould always better be,'twould far, far
better suit a doughty man like me.

Would Aristotle stoop to dress immortal theories, his magnificence
in time-consuming foolishness, iambic triviality?
The problem is I can't refrain from verbal titillation,
words that rhyme I can't disdain, despite their lowly station,
a silly cipher wasting time, poetizing once again.
I'm not like Aristotle then, nor is he quite like me.

In all his works I've only found a catchy phrase or two
of which the composition sticks, of which I can't let go
because unconscious elegance has found its way out through
the density of lofty thought, the brilliant prose he knew.
I guess I'm satisfied to be the lowly poetizing me,
happy with a matching word, some anapestic humor
unconcerned with Aristotle's prose, the grand solemnity
of some lengthy disquisition he could shorten.

I love to sing a rising strophe born with a helpless tear,
I love to plumb, to sound the depths of feelings I now feed on,
feelings never felt before—in words I now can hear,
and if they chance in rhyme to come, approve the composition.

You should read my stuff, Aristotle.

The Unenclosed All, the Strangeness
of 'Locality'

Can one speak of locality in infinite space,
where the word *space*, and even perhaps
the word *infinite* are absurdities?

Given an intelligent being 'somewhere' in
the Unenclosed, would he not suppose himself
—like Aristotle—to be in its center?

But having no shape, can infinity have a center
or any other position presupposing shape?
Apparently not.

Any 'center' or 'location' in the Unenclosed
would be a delusion, the comforting delusion of a
pre-Copernican being.

What about a 3-D Cartesian coordinate with zero at the position
of an intelligent being. Would this not project 1/4 of infinity?
But this would assume being at the center too. And there **is** no center.

And given the inevitability of other foolish geometers throughout infinity,
no single coordinate system could be universally definitive. Infinity
would be a lacework of random coordinate systems.

Early on, Bruno and Crescas conceived of the infinite Unenclosed All as encompassing all that exists or can be imagined. It led Bruno to the stake and Crescas to secret heresy. It leads me to a fascinated incredulity.

Foolishness

When I think "Well that was foolish" can I opt to bless that too,
remembering my immortal father used to do that too?
He'd say "If a good man stumbles on his way he gets up, doesn't halt.
If he's no reason to feel guilty, well, he's just not worth his salt.
This thought mitigates some errors I feel obliged to commit:
If they abound, I'll just cut down, not overdoing it.
My dad would say "Yes, you're my son, your indiscretions small,
'twould make my preacher father swear if he'd known me at all."

How I'd Like to Die

I considered how I'd like to die…
'twas on a grassy slope
with friends beneath a starry sky,
the universe my hope.

But then I had a different thought,
that I was ever there
floating 'cross the universe
or dreaming I was there.

I'd seen an old abandoned mine,
none knew how far it goes.
If I were there at dying time
and I were trapped alone,

I could reflect alone we're born,
alone we die again.
In this dark mine I'm not forlorn.
In fact I'm home again.

My Weird Love Life

A strange thing happens to me
if by some goddess I'd be worshiped:
that when she does, it cheapens her
and turns her into porridge
on which I look with new disdain,
my heart set on new forage,
some queen I'm sure is better than
the one that now can bore me.
Perhaps some new ideal I'll find,
ambrosia to restore me,
some prize for me to throw away
when her fingernails have torn me.
Happy thought.
I'll cast her on the growing heap
of goddess ladies that I've sought,
all ones I'm sure I want to keep,
and disappointed when they're not.
Now I have a peasant girl
who thinks I'm just a clod,
she thinks I'm commoner than dirt,
I think she's almost God.

Awakening

Thinking about my little life,
how slowly it's been straightened
from turmoil, from mindless strife
just recently awakened,

What moves me now is thinking how
good folks were kind to me.
I've never been like them somehow,
or relished how they raised me.

They all had their troubles too,
disappointments, sorrow.
It didn't matter what I'd do,
they'd forgive me on the morrow.
They must have loved me as I was,
they tried to make me happy
when all I wanted—it still is—
is going on inside me.

Only now can I see how
my debt I'll never pay
to those kind folks, as I see now
are still raising me today.

The Secret of Secrets

If I could penetrate the universe we see,
if I could penetrate beyond all that seems to be,
into perfect nothingness,
the theoretic nothingness that everything is in,
the utter blackness, vacuum, cold, where nothing's to be seen,
if I could somehow be there where black emptiness is all,
where up or down cannot be found, there's nowhere you can fall;
if I could describe pure nothingness, where not a thing is there,
where infinity, eternity are just the latest joke,
Who would think a man could grasp the timeless everywhere,
what never changes, always is, a secret I won't share.
I'll tell my wife I have to take a nap here in my chair.
And in this way indulge in chair cosmology.
Given that infinity is infinity, and I am alone somewhere in it...
Let's say I conceive of a straight line running just past me,
extending infinitely to the right and infinitely to the left.
Since it is not unreasonable so far as I can see, that
even as measureless distance goes,
math works: infinity equals infinity.
Assuming this is so, if I snip the line
I will be snipping infinity in half.
But suppose an intelligent being elsewhere in the void
were to do the same thing.
Would that not indicate
lopsidedness in infinity?
Huh—a mutually disruptive situation,
a solipsistic bifurcation?
Either locus, of course, would assume

infinity as a boundary condition,
which of course it would seem to be.
But as Bruno pointed out, infinite space can have no shape whatever.
And nothing without a shape can have a center
or in fact a position anywhere
with respect to the whole thing,
there being no "whole thing"...
So then how can we speak of
being anywhere at all with reference
to where we are quite sure we are?
-to where we are now certain we must be?
This looks like a problem for nihilists.
Still, is it not a problem to avoid thinking
of infinity in one direction as not equaling infinity
in the other? Others have suspected that
infinity is nothing whatever since it can't be defined.
Can we leave it at that?
Yet we know in some sense it has to be something.
Aristotle puzzled about this too.
Disgustingly, he too concluded that infinity doesn't exist.
I think he knew he was begging the question.
Yet does not this eternal emptiness exist because I see it,
the solipsistic all there is evidently starts with me.
Is it different for a praying mantis praying in a tree?
when there's no fly or any bug distraction from his prayer?
Does he not define the center of his own infinity?
And if a bird should pluck him from his altar on the branch,
the bird would think it nothing to ingest eternity,
along with chubby breakfast worms already found by chance.
Somewhere I see within this bird the universe has turned
into an offering, warm ordure, an awesome magisterial
kerplop 'bove my left ear.
I'd be pretty sure of that.

Admission

If I've made firm the bitter lesson that I can't stop myself
from drinking 'til I'm courting hell, forsaking wife and wealth,
once again the past has told me I'm a fool to take a drink,
doesn't matter what resolve I make or what I maybe think.
The strange thing is as long as I'm sure of my inner peril,
as long as I do not deny my heart and soul are feral,
as long as I admit that my unconscious tendency
is permanent, has always been, is now, will ever be
oblivion, sweet nothingness, the dark deep of the sea.
My confidence is weakness, an embraced proclivity
to consign my soul to where I can abandon being me.
I embrace this inner peril as the weapon that I have,
the boldest truth, the kindest ruth my little soul to lave;
so when Jack Daniels calls my name, I know that I'm not strong,
I've strength to say "Just not today. I have to move along."
Thank you Lord, I know you know
I can't do this by myself.

Honors

Aristotle pointed out
that men pursue honor for three reasons:
political gain, as a stepping stone to power;
material gain, as a stepping stone to wealth;
and most interestingly,
for *confirmation of their worth*.
His incidental reflection on the latter
is memorable and poignant.
He said: a complete man
with no need of external validation
will accept honors bestowed on him
anyway, as a courtesy,
inasmuch as honors
are the best folks have to offer.
Could there be a more
arch and condescending response?
Might he not have said the same of love?

Prolixity

Prolix, prolix, prolix, I've always liked that word,
it's short for lengthy tedium, as short as any heard.
And where 'er you find it, you know one's taken leave
to measure some unending verse with his pajama sleeve.

My lines are pretty pithy now, no prolix lines for me,
Where 'er I see an extra word, I place it on a tee.
But needing consolation from an extra word or two
I sneak one in and clear my throat, to see if that will do.

Peace

Gentle, cold, the breeze is stirring,
the flannel shirt I'm wearing's not enough;
yet I'm sitting stolid—getting colder, staring
at the sidewalk here from 30 stories up.

I embrace the mother that has always loved me,
my father surely always loved me too,
my wife would smile and try to make me happy,
but strangely far away from me was all the good I knew.

For in my soul a stillness always beckoned,
a quiet more than quiet here on earth,
the gentleness, the silence that I've looked on
that's never been my portion since my birth.

I've had this little courage in me hiding,
so little effort now to scoot a bit,
and feel the breeze, it's like my dream of flying,
I won't even know it when I hit.

The Insight

What you shared
about the recent insight that
"washed over you like a wave,"
that I have changed—that so many of my pursuits
are now solitary—
that you still want
the romance and togetherness
of our early days…

that I alone have changed…
…that because I am not likely to change,
you will try to accept me as I am.

When I think of this
I experience
a warmth and tenderness toward you
I have not felt for a long time.

Unknown and Unregarded

a'Kempis' book lies on the table just beside my bed.
Of all the things I've read in it the best thing that he said
was "to be unknown and unregarded is the finest thing to know,
to be lowly, humble hearted, unconcerned with worldly show."

I can't help but to remember a'Kempis' solemn verse
when I think of what a speck we are in this vast universe.
Do we not smile at politicians and understand their game,
or salvation-hawking preachers always itching for more fame?

A sage has said that even if the whole world knew his name,
memory's for a moment, like a falling drop of rain.
It's as though one heady earthworm grew more famous than another,
wiser worms make do with their own thoughts,
with fame they needn't bother.

So why should this sage wisdom have such appeal for me?
Wisdom wasn't how I started, acclaim was my ideal.
I thought that fame would prove my worth, my secret stainless steel.
But when I got a bit of fame, a bit of acclamation,

I made mistakes, became a fool, I reaped humiliation.
So now somewhat recovered from the little fame I'd got,
I'm thankful for what I've become, I'm glad for what I'm not.

I'm happy dressed in denim now, happy planting trees.
I'm famous in my neighborhood for perfect black-eyed peas.
But I've kept all that I've written, it's up there on a shelf,
and I still know I'm wonderful—but keep it to myself.

My Righteousness

My righteousness is minimal
but often it will do
as long as I'm not criminal
it will see me through.

I'm sober, sane and safe today,
I say a prayer or two.
I have a few infractions yet,
excusable and few.

My countenance can pass for good,
my friends approve me too,
approval serves me like a food,
approbation too.

So if my scant integrity
can save me from a fall
eulogies are sure to please
this man with merits small.

I still can write a doggerel verse
that satisfaction brings.
Even Shakespeare wrote some worse
—some trite unpublished things.

Perhaps he too, like me and you
had slightly tarnished wings,
though n'er so high a mortal flew
on low unchurchly things.

Morning Thoughts

Mornings sitting in the dark
I watch my neighbor's window,
his television's like a star
changing channels, flickering so.

I read his channel surfing
until he thinks it's time to go,
his window quickly dark'ning.

Then he backs his pickup out,
always carefully and slow.
In the street he turns about,
I'm pretty sure where he will go.

But while I watch his flick'ring light
it may occur to me
his television's like my light
that changes channels constantly.

And I won't know when it goes out
and darkens suddenly.
I just know when it goes out
I'll not be watching sleepily.
No pickup will be backing out
or coming home again.

Eternity Again

Time has no beginning
nor can it have an end.
Though I don't understand it yet,
eternity's my friend.
It tells me I'm a witness to
unknown reality,
a diorama vast and dark,
the true chronology,
the only real significance
beyond what we can see.
If I were full aware of this
I might a preacher be.
I'd tell my congregation how
our little 'now' stands as a surety
for what remains ungraspable,
this backdrop we inhabit,
the meaningless temporal word
pronounced e-ter-ni-ty;
how it goes both ways forever,
how it's never heard of time,
how it laughs across infinity,
laughs at the confusion
it makes on the human mind.
I see that I'm a cipher,
my mind I know is small,
yet I inhabit everything,
the in-dub-itable All.
But…it's a fair guess

God Himself can't understand the mess he created.
The congregation will now rise
and turn to page...uh...
three hundred thousand forty-five.

Silence

Continuing in silence
I hear a symphony,
the silence of the universe,
the silence of a tree,
the silence of her shining eyes,
that haunt my memory;

the silence of the ocean depths,
the ships, the stalwart sailors
where silent on the bottom rest
their statues in the sediment,
still forevermore.

May the symphony I hear
that lifts my magic carpet
surround me with a silence rare
where any choir would forfeit
the most inspired sound.

Let me choose the stillness then
a silent dreamless sleep
that moves unmoving,
hears unhearing,
sharing what the silence keeps.

Morning Prayer

Keep me sober, sane and safe today,
even with the flow,
out of trouble, rancor, fray,
constantly to know
a peace beyond my understanding
anchoring my soul,
where even in the lions' den
I'll find myself still bold.

So let me murmur 'thank you'
a hundred times today.
If humor can be managed too,
some of that would be okay.

The Big Bang

The Big Bang didn't make a sound,
it was silent as a kitten's nap,
an impenetrable darkness where
all that is, (around here),
exploded outward
in c-exceeding speed,
reaching exponential distances,
a picosecond's deed.
Dense radiating fragments
of unassembled strings
were the stuff of this explosion,
the only things alive
in that brief homesteading moment.

After strings assembled
in ten thousand years or more
just the thing that hungry quarks,
those early sharks,
had long been waiting for.
In no time three quarks combined
and protons popped up everywhere;
these condensing made a mist
a fog of aggregations,
a universe each speck of mist
our best simulations
cannot fathom.
Who would guess Beethoven
was being made?

Perspective

I often visit,
I often go back
to the region where nothing remains.
On all that is, it's my final attack,
it's where I don't mind if I'm slightly insane.
Beyond Hubble volumes, a number of them
and universe clusters nearby
I breathe in the vacuum, my infinite den,
where I see all that is
is a carnival lie.
It's out in this darkness I finally see
infinity's just a bit smaller,
eternity's quick, a wing beat of a bee.
Big Bangs are a hum that's imagined,
a silent perdurable soliloquy.
As I float here and ponder my peregrinations
a problem arises—it's probably moot:
to see the real meaning of civilizations,
of life and death struggles, can it be acute
to strain for a cause, to die for a passion
in infinite time? What's the rhyme or the reason
when you're far away in the infinite nothing;
will justice and right still be on the line?
McCarthy of course would say yes.

Norm

Norm's first cabin had no windows,
didn't have a door,
its only means of access
was a tunnel 'neath the floor,
an entrance neatly hidden.

Its only social niceties
were gun slits in the walls,
features hardly aimed to please
a social folderol.

With a locked gate and warning signs
for pious Jehovah's Witnesses
and others who might come,
Norm would sit and read Thoreau,
and, in fear of patriotic citizens,
would write of Viet Nam,
how the Navy soiled him
and all that he'd been taught,
how the nation shamed him,
made him hide his uniform,
his beautiful steel tail hook,
his PTSD nightmares,
his PTSD thought.

Norm and I were instant friends
when I moved to town.
He might have heard unspoken things,
opinions I kept down.

The most surprising thing any
brand new friend has said,
was "Can I call you every morning—when you're up and out of bed."
He said, "Could we read together about
what you said tonight,
the causes of hysteria,
the terror, terror, terror
from which I flee at night?

So every morning for three years,
when we were both in town
we read Freud and Breuer
we inventoried fears
on the telephone.

When Norm's wife died
he moved to a warmer clime
He still calls me now and then,
he's found a lovely wife.
His cabin he won't see again.
(story continued...)

Hallowed Ground

The suspicion that eternity is real,
if ungraspable, creates the thought
that all I see,
the rocks and trees,
everything I feel
has been perfected
at incalculable cost,
with incalculable care
in an unplanned eternity
lost to comprehension.

The chance that time and happenstance
have done this can't detract
when I see the cunning crafting
of a careful, careless act
made more holy
by the premeditation that it lacked,
It bathes me in the reverence
Moses must have found
listening to the silent dust:
"Take off your shoes,
you stand on holy ground."

The passing cars and busy people—
who would suppose that all we see
is something priceless, never seen,
the unexpected love-child,
the unheard music of a deaf eternity.

Consciousness

Consciousness, the everything
that Huxley thought unknown;
he called it man's great mystery,
a genie from a bottle grown.
This unaware baseline assumption,
this always present festival
creating everything we see
(we think death is like the rest,
just not cognitively blest);
but as we can clearly see
our godlike trait is equally
in fish, insects, bacteria,
creatures that know how to flee—of living things the panoply,
even moss and living trees,
if they have a sense of happiness.
So the mystery of consciousness
must be common in the universe,
circling many stars we see, maybe many more.
I think that consciousness is common,
this consciousness
our telescopes are looking for,
and no matter if we smarter get,
with consciousness our single tool
it remains a mystery
ungrasped, unanalyzed as yet.

Recliner Thoughts

There's a fear that confounds me
as I'm sitting here
in the safety of my leather
overstuffed reclining chair.
Ready missiles could fly,
the economy tank,
my dear wife could die,
I could have a Thanksgiving
with nothing to thank.
And if a chance bolide,
say twelve miles in breadth,
should hit in the oceans,
all the world's coastlines
were swallowed in death,
we lucky remaining
would die in the dust.
Yet I'm sitting here
in my overstuffed chair
horrified 'spite my soft situation.
It just happens sometimes,
that my foreboding rhymes,
and I find myself quaking, afraid of the air.
To find consolation I'll read Solzhenitsyn,
the Gulag soothes and induces content.
or I'll slowly digest Dostoevsky's

seven years in the House of the Dead.
I'll even Jonathan Edwards applaud,
convicted and sentenced, alas, what a wretch!
in the slough of desolation, despond,
gripped tight in the Hands of an Angry God.
Otherwise I'm pretty cheerful.

Counterclockwise

I'm a counterclockwise person,
rotate backward as I rhyme;
and in this way undo the day
and manufacture time.

My friends are counterclockwise too.
We watch the world unravel.
We don't repent, we're tolerant,
we seldom bang the gavel.

And when the common end has come
—the clockwise crowd in fear and doubt—
we'll be laughing, having fun,
we'll just be starting out.

Thank You

If I think to think 'Thank you' for little successes,
even sometimes for small troubles I have,
an impromptu 'thank you' often will undue
any upsetting disturbance I have.

If I think to think 'Thank you' in moments of stress,
it banishes most of my tension;
it helps, even dispels, my unhappiness,
releasing imagination.

"Thank you' I've never regretted to whisper
among other words I regret.
Whatever I'm doing is lighter and better;
it's the best prayer I've found yet.

This prayer is a secret redoubtable way
to disarm my challenges many;
any darkness of countenance light will allay,
and of troubles I'll have hardly any.

Thank you for teaching this one needful prayer,
for teaching the magic of thinking
this effortless thought that can go anywhere.
Thank you, I thank you for my thank you prayer

Even So...

A one-millimeter pinhead is roughly
a trillion (1,000,000,000,000)
times larger than a proton.
If the earth were that proton,
that proton-earth would yet be
ten million times larger than me.
The earth is ten billion times
larger than a pinhead.
The galaxy is a hundred
trillion times larger than the earth.
The visible universe is
twenty thousand times
larger than the galaxy.
The unseen universe
is thought to be a trillion trillion
times larger than the universe we see.
So at a hundred and forty pounds, I am
ten million trillion trillion
trillion trillion trillionths
of the local universe,
itself an invisible speck in infinity.
Even so, I bump into things in my shop.

Drying Up

I'm like a well becoming dry,
solidifying mud—No feelings, thoughts to make me cry,
no swelling inspiration.
There's so much I have to tell,
such literary riches.
But I just sit here, chew my cud;
wandering in the ditches
of disgusting ennui.
The muse will have to find me—if there is a muse indeed—
this languid lump, this lifeless stump
that doesn't give a shoot—constrained to wait. But hesitate…
there may be life within.
Perhaps some anapestic prose
will piddle from my pen.
Yeah.

Beethoven and His Father

Listen to his outpouring of spirit!
Do I understand Beethoven's
wringing out of unimagined depths?
Whence this eruption of unheard beauty?
His father, a drunken Salieri,
knew him as infinitely superior,
loved and hated him.
The boy felt the love and hate,
but relished the hate and rage.
His father would come home drunk,
wake him and tell him to play,
Gladly shunning sleep,
the boy in joyful dominance
with unplanned innovations
would savage his father's heart,
adding tears to his drunkenness.
Overcome, his father would beg him to stop,
but he wouldn't until he was beaten.
Even then Beethoven knew
he was overcoming Odin.
So it was all his life,
composing his unstoppable music.
I see Odin standing behind him drunk,
weeping, begging him to stop.
Beethoven, triumphant, is still saying
No, listen to this!

Even in those last days when he was poor, ill,
stone deaf, wretchedly housed, utterly alone,
Odin was still standing behind him drunk,
weeping, begging him to stop.
Yet Beethoven would say, and forever says
No! Listen to this! Listen!

Finland

Finns are quiet and savage.
Everybody smokes, drives ninety.
The trees are holy and unlike other trees,
the marshes sullen, full of sullen weeds,
yet they too bring tears to the eyes of a Finn.
Finns invent their own hinges,
rig their houses like ships.
Taciturn, they roll naked in the snow.
The Russians have learned not to invade.
Sibelius, however loud, is quiet
as a slow walk by a still lake,
unexcitable as the boulders
on the northern coast.
The Finns translate other languages,
yet no one can translate theirs.
Even when pleased, a Finn
will politely refrain from smiling.

Walnut Street

When I'm quiet in my room,
content in my library,
I'm sure I know a thing or two,
my books can make me merry.

Imagining some worldly fame,
with being known and mighty,
then wishing I could be the same,
my lamp burning as brightly
as in the past.

I enjoy being a recluse where
only friends can find me,
the simplest of simple men;
none of the neighbors mind me.
Where I invade the universe,
where I can ride the clouds and sky,
where I can sometimes pen a verse
oblivious, not wondering why.

I'm sure advantage can't be had
with noisy proclamation,
my fun is peace, not being sad
about my situation.

Everything is all the same
among us conscious beings,
I know that accolades and fame,
would stop these inner seeings.

Nighttime darkness, slow sunrise,
now serve to satisfy me,
I'm happy just a book to ply,
some challenging philosophy
like that of Schopenhauer.

I sometimes linger in the void,
in perfect darkness waiting
and try to sense Almighty God,
creation in the making.

The God I've found is nothingness,
going on forever.
In endless void incredulous,
timeless infinity,
a place I cannot fathom,
or haven't fathomed yet.

The strangest place my thoughts can go,
the void from which I cannot roam,
is like the house on Walnut Street
I used to call my home.

Why this endless fascination
with a dark infinity,
is it imagination,
my protons' destination,
the final rest, the zero sum,
the nothing left of me?

I find what I've been searching for—the place I've always been,
where universes playthings are
like dust grains in the wind.

Yet even here beyond the stars
I still can see my old address
on Walnut Street,
the brick house on the corner.

Is it a star, a galaxy
that mars my meditation?
Could it be the memory
of my mother's smile?

Could it be the sadness
I felt when I was twelve,
the momentary gladness
hopping over curbs
with the Schwinn that I rebuilt?

In the furthest reaches,
in the darkness of the void,
I see I cannot leave
the house on Walnut Street.

Even here beyond the stars,
something clings to Walnut Street.
Did I hear a music there,
some silly tune I must repeat
throughout eternity?

The World (Inchoate Meter)

Awareness of the world is something
that I haven't got.
I'm satisfied with smaller things.
I concentrate on cadence while I'm stitching up a sock
(a favorite pair; one with a growing hole).
I'm becoming more content
with what I am and what I'm not.
I follow Schopenhauer.
I think he said a lot,
namely that the world was his idea.
I can fix it like my sock,
a clever stitch or two
and bingo, good as new,
just like my fav'rite argyle sock.

Criticizing

If I criticize my coupon-clipping wife
for spending too much money
and then look around at the poor little life,
the things I've provided convict me.

The blessing is she's faithful and well satisfied.
So I'm caught in my error, and suddenly sad,
unworthy to have such a woman,
unworthy the love of this woman

At Home Here

I am the stuff of supernovae.
Do my equations tell
upon the fabric where I dwell?
How is it I contrive to know
the universe I see?
Is my fond imagination just audacity—in this starry cathedral
pondering a place for me?

No! I am the stuff of supernovae!
It is correct I plot to plot
trajectories and just how far
an asteroid will miss us.
I am not a stranger here,
a supernova was my womb.
How is it we think that we can see
beyond this universe of stars
into the nothingness beyond,
climb about infinity
the way a child plays in the park?
An exploding star the womb of me.
The Big Bang is my pedigree.
The ideas here are two: one
is that my mind is at home here
like a baby duck in water;
every fiber is a native of this place.

I am a worthy scion
of all that is and isn't.
I've never been this old I've said.
So I suppose someday I'll say
I've never been this dead.

Norm (Continued)

I hadn't met this unusual man,
but one evening after I mentioned
that PTSD was called male hysteria in 1918,
he came over and asked "Can I call you every morning?"

He called each morning for three years—until his wife died.
We read much of Freud, The Golden Bough and whatnot.
He told me a lot about himself.
Still small enough to sit on his mother's lap,
Shakespeare, The Wealth of Nations, and other attention getters
were read. His father was a wounded WWII vet.

Norm had been a squadron commander on the Coral Sea.
Coming home from Viet Nam he survived Jane Fonda,
mostly by marrying an Ojibwa, holing up, reading Thoreau,
drinking and writing songs.

As a kid, Norm had a toy aircraft carrier.
On his sixth birthday six neighbor kids came over.
He wore the sailor suit his mother had bought him.
For his birthday cake she had made an aircraft carrier.
It had to be baked in two sections. It had a broad deck,
a conning tower, fighter planes and six candles.
The kids sang Happy Birthday. She lit the candles.

It was night off the Gulf of Tonkin, monsoon winds, heavy seas.
Could he land his crippled A4 jet
on the pitching rising deck? Cold sweat!
The tail hook caught. The neighbor kids were singing.
His beautiful mother, now long dead,
stood overhead lighting candles.

Valentine

It's best to let your dear wife come
and sue for your affection,
than play the slavish dunce and run,
soliciting attention.

It's best to be a calm oak tree wrapped in thought, philosophy,
content with your own company.

The best of wives has come to you,
the perfect wife you'd never pick
if it were left to you.

A woman's choice is always best.
Then you can smile your inward smile
and know yourself more clever while
a captive of the wench.

Being Nothing

I'll be nothing, see nothing,
sample the void,
care nothing, bear nothing,
happ'ly destroyed.

A moment eternal,
always with me,
enduring, supernal.
I finally can see
the fusslessness, nothingness
beckoning me.

Like granite awaiting
its crumbling to dust,
I see I'm ablating,
I see that I must.

That Nothing's forever.
I'm happy I'm not
immortal, enduring
malodorous rot.

What a place I'll achieve!
The enveloping void!
The finest of comforts,
that can't be destroyed,
a dreamless perdurable peace.

The Emperor Concerto

The sweetest scent my mother had—it surely was her breast—
now comes from this adagio so sad,
a murmur fainter than the rest,
the fully perfect world I've had.
I hardly know what I have found.
I smell the music, know it's there.
It's there, it's there, I know it's there
like Mole discovering his home,
yet obliged to keep on moving.
If only I can know it's there
I'll wrap myself in knowing.

Did I see, touch, taste and smell
her milk-wet breast, reveling in love,
enchanted by her song?
Beethoven surely knew it too,
the sight, the touch, the taste of God
the song divine he listened to?
The song his mother sang?
For him too this lullaby too sad for words,
in his infant tissues rang.

This surely was my mother's song,
my secret of survival.
I didn't know I knew it,
yet I've known it all along.

For this forgotten music smell
I've searched so hungrily,
not knowing that I know it well.
Her leaking breast a god to me
in this piano music.

A Tough Texas Mother

Not once in her childhood,
not once in her life,
did her mother say I love you.
O yes, there was once
those words came through
just as she died
in the arms of her loving daughter.
I'll never understand the human heart.

Those Who Would Love Me

Maimonides would love me
for immersing myself in the Mishnah Torah
'til I found his incomparable humor.
Ibn Ezra would love me
for understanding his discomfort.
Elie Wiesel would love me
for seeing his beautiful face,
his skin and bones at Auschwitz.
Leo Strauss would love me
for learning so well to read between the lines.
Even that Galilean boy
would love me for understanding
his willing penury.

From the First Page of Spinoza's Treatise on the Emendation of the Intellect

I read this at age thirty when I had failed in the ordinary world and achieved nothing in any other. This first published passage of Spinoza became a permanent fixture with me. I include a more recent marginal comment in the new edition of Samuel Shirley.

After experience had taught me the hollowness and futility of everything that is ordinarily encountered in daily life, and I realized that all the things which were the source and object of my anxiety held nothing of good or evil in themselves save insofar as the mind was influenced by them, I resolved at length to enquire whether there existed a true good, one which was capable of communicating itself and could alone affect the mind to the exclusion of all else, whether, in fact, there was something whose discovery and acquisition would afford me a continuous and supreme joy to all eternity.

I say 'resolved at length', for at first sight it seemed ill-advised to risk the loss of what was certain in the hope of something at that time uncertain. I could well see the advantages that derive from honor and wealth, and that I would be forced to abandon their quest if I were to devote myself to some new and different objective. And if in fact supreme happiness were to be found in the former, I must inevitably fail to attain it, whereas if it did not lie in these objectives and I devoted myself entirely to them, then once again I would lose that highest happiness.

A remarkable statement. How did he know he would 'inevitably fail'? If his failure was inevitable, the 'certain good' spoken of was not certain. Are these 'ordinary goods' actually straw men for Spinoza? What was certain for Spinoza was that he would fail in the ordinary world. I think we may be certain of that too. In any case, this expression of resignation is the most admirable I have ever seen.

Another Masterpiece

Old folks, we nap 'tween two and three.
Then we do some reading, often ancient history,
some text with lots of meaning.
At four we're pretty tired out,
but I've some chores to do,
I have to feed the cats and
scoop their litter boxes too.
Excitement's not our cup of tea, we're satisfied with snoozing,
changing channels on TV, this news stuff's not amusing.
Lawrence Welk, we always found uplifting, happy, soothing.
The status quo, I've come to know,
provides a long-sought refuge now,
the way a checkered, wasted life
has finally, kindly, taught me how, to be.
But… were I another actor in another show,
I'd be the top bull rider in the Cheyenne rodeo.
Sweaty, with bull energy, I'd still spoil for more.
For laughs I'd saunter to the town, then kick in the door
of some two-bit cowboy bar and loudly share:
"I can whip the biggest baddest
mother[expletive] here!" Truth to tell.
Then to ease that introduction
I'd buy everyone a beer, then several more.
After all, that's what bull money's for.
These are things I'd never rue,
like showing some lucky cowgirl
that she can do it too.
But it's now near eight-thirty

and I'm such a sleepyhead.
I'll put on my pajamas,
take my pills and go to bed.
But I'll tell you what, that last bull was a dandy.

Explaining Things

If I could have a moment,
If I could have a word,
I'd tell a different story,
the strangest you have heard.
It's not that I'm so special 'mong the millions that we see;
it's just that I'm a pronoun
in a box I know as me.
I've considered the hypothesis
'reality is real,'
but tend to be a skeptic in the bushes.
I approve of what I feel
and think that all I see
is just quantum observation
that will disappear with me.

This simplifies the universe,
makes it my conception;
it could be better, can't be worse
than glorified deception.
With splendid thoughts here in my box
I manufacture me and you—and everything there is.
I've shared these thoughts in confidence,
I certify they're true.
And if it worries you a bit
that all I've said applies to you,
just mull it over and you'll hit
on solipsism too.
Just keep it to yourself.

Nothing

I'll be nothing, see nothing,
sample the void,
care nothing, bear nothing,
fully destroyed.

The moment's eternal,
always with me,
enduring, supernal,
I finally see.
Fusslessness, nothingness
beckons to me.

Like a rock that is waiting
to crumble to dust,
slowly ablating,
knowing it must.

Nothing's forever
as sure as I'm not
enduring, immortal,
or animal rot.

What a place this enveloping void!
A curious comfort
routinely enjoyed
at the end of Maple Street.

Acumen

I find in my acumen a fine futility,
redress of small-town commonness,
the barnyard self, the bright facade
of barnyard dreams that never came to be.

Seeking a love I'll never have
has made a clown of me.
I know as genuine
my tree house memory,
and the second movement
of Beethoven's seventh symphony.

The conning trail his heart has left,
the universe we share.
Was I an angel in his vacant room,
while near God's chair he stormed
an absent heaven with these lines?

His transfigured resignation resonates in me,
as I listen to these heart-invading lines.
My barnyard self transmutes to gold.
Breathing in these lines, I know I'm not alone.

I was in the air he breathed, fibers in the paper
he used when he composed.

New Speculation

What conclusion can be drawn from the new speculation,
evidential as it is, about our cosmic insignificance?
About the untendentive way of creation and decay?
That infinity after all is real.
And try to grasp the nugatory consequence of time!
A fourteen-billion-year-old photon doesn't need it.
Are all my thoughts, my lifetime, a vaporous illusion,
a Hubble volume I can move with a glass or two of wine?

I remember knowing I owned all I could see
through a crack in the boards of my tree house.
That was dependable tree house reality.
Is it the same with our telescopes,
spying on the universe?

In March I found a hungry cat, took it home with me;
then it ate, began to purr: now it belongs to me.
Could that be the story 'bout the universe and me?
The cat would seem to think so.

To a Christian Lady

Thank you for your pamphlet, your concern for my soul.
I know yours is a path of peace for many, an abiding solace.
Even though an 'infidel', I have this of which you speak, always have had.
This Presence is always with me, somehow guiding every thought and action,
every triumph, angry outburst, every blunder.
It is in every priceless rapture, in everything I make.

This 'What I know' without knowing it
was with David when he leapt that wall,
when he led his men up the drain to found Jerusalem.
This 'What I know' was with Nathan at the side of Sabbati Zevi,
with Leonidas as Xerxes dismembered him,
with Beethoven as he wrote the Seventh Symphony,
with every hara-kiri Kamikaze taking off,
with the myriads who said their last Shema at Auschwitz.

He was with me in blackouts, driving drunk,
watched over such a wretch as me,
orchestrating misery to help
me sober up.
Embraced by all this love, could I not be loyal?

Dissecting Room

I dreamed a nasty little dream,
a dream that wrung my heart: 'twas at the school's dissecting room
to guard the door—my given part.
I felt my face at once grow pale,
inside I fell apart
I saw it was my own dear mother on the donor cart
wheeled I fear like any other
to the grim dissecting room. 'Twas when I saw her kindly face
in recognition nod
I saw the world's a carnival,
there isn't any God.
Another dream that pierced me—it was summer time.
My parents had a party, I was maybe nine.
Outside I heard the laughter,
all the words they spoke.
I listened unprepared to hear
my dear mother laughing at a dirty joke.
In that tiny moment
something in me tore apart. 'Twas if I'd seen in time to come
my mother on that cart
entering the dissecting room.
Her face was twisted with her laughter,
and now she didn't nod.
The world is just a carnival,
there isn't any God.
Then I had a vision I'd never had before
Our maid, our modest Mennonite
her bonnet 'er in place—our white-prayer-bonneted Mennonite girl

315

Hilda, our maid. I was thirteen,
I'm still in love with her.
She stood alone in her ankle-length dress
at the edge of a boxing ring.
The crowd was shouting "Undress, undress!"
You could hear a drunken chorus sing.
I looked away, it made me sick,
I saw her hips start moving.
(But for my part she didn't move—just stood there in her homemade dress.)
The crowd burst into happiness,
whistling, starting to applaud.
She shyly smiled, grew willing then
to pacify the crowd.
Docile, gracious and serene,
the loveliest woman I'd ever seen.
in her white prayer bonnet
and her homemade cotton dress
carried on that cold grey cart.
An anatomist there would name each part,
displaying great anatomical art,
showing them how to dissect a Mennonite lady.
I knew some of the students there
who would ogle a specimen so fair
their hyena scalpels waiting
their watching teacher's nod.
The world is just a carnival,
there isn't any God.

These iconic women were innocent of offense, but I required that they offend before being taken to the dissecting room. Despite these necessary offenses, the horror felt at their potential dissection recognized their lack of blemish. The case of the Mennonite girl, interestingly, was more devastating than that of my mother. The overall theme would seem to be the sanctity of women. Were they, like God's people, required to "offend" before being taken to Auschwitz?

In Defense of Sigmund Freud

Sigmund Freud remains one of the most learned and original scientists, physicians, and philosophers who have ever lived.

In his time, he was unique in recognizing the importance of sexual matters in neurosis and therapy, for which the ignorant continue to this day to join in speaking out against his name. In my experience, these derogations come from people who have not read one line of the twenty-four volumes of his writings.

He was a man of the broadest range of interests and scholarship. Familiar with Shakespeare, Goethe, and Dostoevsky, he formulated foundational theories of their biographical development. He contributed fascinating understandings of Sophocles and Leonardo. He wrote on the formation of religions and civilization. His recognition of the unconscious mind in *The Interpretation of Dreams* was ground-breaking worldwide. It was also, incidentally, a stimulus to the development of art in Vienna in the early twentieth century.

Freud's importance in intellectual history and psychology continues to grow. He may be reasonably regarded as having contributed more to the understanding of human beings than any one man who has ever lived. He continues worthy of a lifetime of study. In my opinion, his *Interpretation of Dreams* alone ranks him with Aristotle, Newton, and Copernicus. Few know that he and Einstein collaborated in trying to find an effective deterrent to war. To join in the popular disparagement of him is to broadcast one's ignorance.

Would That I Could See...(1)

Would that I could see
from somewhere we're sure exists
some little way into infinity,
the all or most of what there is,
especially the tiny bit wherein
our galaxy's a part.

Would that I could understand
in a way I never have
the silliness of pride,
the glory of a knave,
insignificance historified,
the ultra-insignificance of man.

Would that I could see
the microscopic speck I am
in a microscopic galaxy
in a universe that soon won't be
in existence that much longer.

Would that I could see
what surely
waits beyond it all,
a darkness where no one can see,
waiting there so patiently.
It's possible all this I'll see
some day if I'm lucky.

But I just now remember the huge bacterium,
I clearly saw, the Bacillus megaterium,
autonomous, a very god withal, cruising like a submarine
beneath a coverslip.

God! I'd love to be like him in my inner self,
the essence of an authentic majesty
that knows the universe was made
for the likes of you and me.

Would That I Could See...(2)

Would that I could see
an ultramicroscopic way into infinity.
Would our universe would stay
maybe a microsecond longer
either way in virginal eternity,
virginal, untouched eternity.
Could there be an endless story
in a Planck-length span of time,
that would raise excessive laughter,
but have parts 'twere held sublime
by any listener?
Would that I could glimpse
the whole cosmogenic plan, let's say,
as it becomes and disappears
in one over google squared a picosecond times
or even some much slower pace that rhymes.
If these peregrinations could glimpse eternity,
glimpse what must be going on
in our ultramicroscopic part of infinity,
we could do some calculations,
make sagacious estimations,
get a bug's view of creation
any time we have to wait
like this
with our melting ice cream
in a grocery line.

A Peaceful Dream Listening to Sibelius

The strangest horse, the strangest man
in mountains high, amid a grassy meadow.
No one would guess how they had come
to this epiphanic place,
but they were here somehow,
in this dream meadow walking.
The sun was high, the clouds were still,
'twas as if the air were talking, saying
"The very air, the clouds, the massive rocks,
the wilderness, the friendly silence here,
the horse's neck, the still sunshine,
that worn-out flannel shirt of mine…"
When Sibelius began to sound his
melancholy strains
the purr of distant thunder came,
like the whisper of a woodchuck's feet
running 'cross the ground.
Far away the horse could see the
purple streaks of rain.
Distant lightning winked a greeting.
We both knew why we'd come.
The fading sound of flutes was there,
encouraging the breeze;
the flutes kept time with the sound
of meadow grass upon the horse's knees.
Such a lovely, lasting dream of peace!
But it was time to turn around.

Mystics

A mystic's opinions differ
from those of an orthodox peer.
They need not seek God
for they've already found
his presence is already near,
a majesty they'd be embarrassed to fear.
They'll take off their shoes the better to see,
fast to have a full belly,
in study may weep in his embrace,
for only a moment with him to be.
Any suffering they know as an undeserved grace,
a promise of what is and what is to be.

When such a mystic
at length has grown old,
having achieved perfection,
he just might sport a long gray beard,
his portable prehistoric abode
and maybe ride a Harley Davidson
humming Hallelujah down the road.

The Seventh Symphony

The 2nd movement of the Seventh Symphony—as I read it—consists in its beat of large sections of sustained dactylic hexameter overlain (strangely it would seem) by iambic pentameter—an arrangement one might think awkward in a poem.
But to dabble with this form, stressed syllables bolded:

How on earth would this look?
—verses offset to form an off'ring of that style?
Pulse pulse pulse pulse pulse
pulse pulse pulse pulse pulse…
these syncopated lines beguiled me so…
…then with a thump thump thump thump thump…always to follow…
But what could match the splendor
of Beethoven's inspiration wild?
Only angels singing in the clouds,
Only choruses of angels in the sky.
The universe was begging for
this strange man to be born,
to compose, all too quickly live and die.
Who of us can see him pouring out his soul
upon that consecrated page?
I can hardly listen to this more than moving music
without importing of his passion just enough to make me weep,
happy tears to see, to hear, to feel,
to know this man will never die,
and something in me joins him,
some small part that will not die.

Closing the Prayer Book

Early in his first book on Jewish mysticism, Gershom Scholem—who says very little about the mystical "state"—wrote: "Nothing seems to me to express better the distance [i.e., the nearness possible] between God and man, than the Hebrew term... *devekuth*, which signifies "adhesion" or "being joined"... to God. This is regarded as the ultimate goal of religious perfection. *Devekuth* can be ecstasy, but its meaning is far more comprehensive. It is a perpetual being-with-God, an intimate union and conformity of the human and the divine will."

Reading this now makes me reflect on a certain experience I once had. When I knew I was lost, I made a place behind a curtain in our cellar where I could read. After immersing myself in Maimonides and other rabbinic giants for a few years, I began to spend time every morning and night reading the Hertz prayer book. It often became a sweet, distinctly hypnotic exercise for me. I came to know the book so well that I would follow a discovered sequence of readings that would after some unknown length of time produce a trance-like state.

One day after these readings, as I closed the prayer book, I had a moment of what Scholem describes as "*devekuth*", of "being with God." Because I was bathed for a moment in the knowledge that I had found all I needed, the sufficiency, all I had looked for of worth. I muttered, "Ah...

A Ouija Fix

A widow won a Ouija board
in Bingo Parlor play.
Her Ouija board she soon adored,
she Ouija Ouija'd every day,
she would Ouija when she could.
She Ouija'd every Wednesday,
when she shouldn't, when she should;
she called it work, she called it play,
She Ouija'd night, she Ouija'd day,
she now puts on a Ouija smile,
she walks a Ouija Ouija way
some shore-leave sailor to beguile,
waylaying him her Ouija way.
her Ouija, Ouija, Ouija way.
It happens I'm a Ouija man,
I Ouija Wednesdays when I can.
I spied her on one Ouija day,
I thought I'd be her Ouija prey.
But
her Ouija board was put away,
she couldn't seem to make it play,
or so she winked and told me.
I knew I should have walked away,
but she persuaded me to stay
and see if I could fix her Ouija board.

Cardboard Roses

A homeless man I know bought roses
from cardboard $1s he swore he'd save.
He didn't say what they were for,
But knowing him I'm pretty sure
he walked up 3rd
and put them on his mother's grave.

Big Place, Big Numbers

A recent notation in cosmology is the 'google',
ten to the one hundredth power. A google thus is
ten thousand trillion trillion trillion trillion
trillion trillion trillion trillion. If a google were raised to the google power,
it could be expressed by chanting the above string of trillions
a trillion trillion trillion trillion trillion trillion trillion trillion
times. If some imaginary device were to pronounce all the zeroes involved
at the rate of one zero per second (neglecting the fact that there are thirty-one
million seconds per year), it would take 10^{100} years (about the life of our
universe) just to get started. Since serial exponents multiply, the device would
have a trillion trillion trillion trillion trillion trillion trillion trillion years to go,
approximately.
A length of cord just a google to a google of millimeters long
could wrap the known universe thickly like a golf ball
(though I confess I haven't done the calculation).
So let us imagine on the model of a spiral galaxy
a supercluster of galaxy-like forms consisting
of one hundred billion dots,
each dot of which is a cluster
of one hundred billion universes.
The circumference of such a supercluster
by our standards would be big
—might well be a google to a few serial google exponents
not in millimeters but in light years.
This is big. Not only that, but there would have to be an endless number of
such superclusters spiraling slowly with respect to each other.

How slowly would such monster spirals rotate?
Because of their size very slowly; their angular velocity would be,
say, ten to the minus thirty-three seconds every google of years.
However, from the perspective of Eternity
these superclusters would be spinning, laughing at astronomers.

My Dancing Tree

Now the buds, now the leaves,
I think I see the springtime courage
of this wild elm tree
now green, opaque,
blowing in the wind,
the cold, unendurable spring wind.
When there is no doubt
I'm near my final end,
may I chance to see
and know
this intrepid tree is there,
growing still,
sometimes dancing wildly in the wind,
even in the cold, unendurable spring wind,
this little scrawny tree,
dancing as though in syncopation to
Beethoven's Fantasy in C.

Was Beethoven looking out his window
keeping time with branches he could see
leafy branches that seemed to dance in ecstasy
in the cold, unendurable spring wind?
Beethoven too sometimes needed inspiration.

A Fish that Turned into a Horse

A Strange Dream:

On the first clumsy cast near the shore
I hooked a large trout that didn't seem
to struggle as I attached him to
my stringer and carried him
to my friend's cabin.
I hung him from a post on the porch
and expected him to die.
But he wouldn't stop struggling.
My friend said, "I know that fish. See that
indentation on its back? It was a horse
with a broken back that I disposed of in the lake."
I saw the indentation, the metempsychosis
and watched the desperately struggling fish
turn into the horse it had formerly been.
I could not stand to see the horse struggling,
experiencing this torture.
My friend, seeing my discomfort,
brought an ice pick and a hammer
and dispatched the horse, now a fish
that had not ceased to struggle.

I can no more bear to see
the prolonged suffocation of a fish.
I have not been fishing since.

330

Written While Sick

It's like I'm on a little raft
carried out to sea.
Where I go, I cannot know,
I hardly know it's me.

I'm grateful for this little raft
I know was once a tree,
a tree grown tall,
then sawed at last
into boards for me.

It must be my unknowing time,
my time of mystery,
my time for dreaming up a rhyme
while floating out to sea.

My mother still is with me;
she calls 'It's suppertime'
but sees I'm napping on my raft
and making up a rhyme.

All I know is that I go
befriended by the sea,
just floating with no need to know,
just floating out to sea.

A Dark Time

There comes a dark time in my life,
a cold, unfriendly wind that blows
that feeds on some unnoticed strife
and muddies up the stream that flows
from somewhere up above.

It tells me I should stop my work,
just put my tools away.

This dissonance infests my heart
like deli cheese on deli pork
so I myself am trafe today.

But I might be okay to sup
with my friend Sabbati Zevi,
swap conclusions, laugh it up
and find that we agree:
there are only false messiahs.

Situation Ethics

Mucking out my irrigation ditch,
the big square trap that catches weeds and silt,
I realized the tool I needed for the corners
was that big slotted serving spoon
I've seen among the spatulas and meat forks.
But it didn't work.
Right away it bent and the forward rivet broke.
I cleaned it up, but it looked ruined.
I bent it back to approximately the right shape
and snapped the broken rivet into place.
My wife doesn't like me using her stuff
without asking,
so I just left it in the drawer for posterity.
A month later she brought it to me
and said, "This old thing has come undone.
Do you think you could fix it? It really is very nice.
It was one of my grandmother's wedding presents."

With the greatest of care I drilled
and re-riveted this serving spoon.
I got the shape just right.
I was pleased with my work.
When I showed it to my wife for her approval,
she kissed me and said I'd done a perfect job.
I had.

Muse

Her long hair,
her sad smiling eyes,
warm magnetic rivets that
obliterate my natural bent for triviality.
How shall I counter her embarrassed laugh,
her terrible self-consciousness,
her girlish offer of frivolity?
Whatever it was she said
about her bashful flirting
made me wish I'd said
"Maybe we could flirt together
in the dark."
I'm pretty sure she would have said
"Maybe we could."
But have I not had enough of tragic women?
Must I fail the test of a mature,
redoubtable philosophy?
Surely not! A dignified philosopher like me?
I have now long been a mystic,
an illuminate fastened to God's will like a bumper hitch.
Were I now to slink away like Jonah
from her truth-saturated eyes,
from her offered lifeline
of redemption, salvation,
of the pull of gravity itself,
how could I stand guiltless in the Court of Heaven?
Maybe I could take her for an ice cream cone.

Comment on Eternity

To start with, we need one of the biggest numbers now used by cosmologists, a google to a google. A google is ten raised to the one hundredth power. To review how exponents work, think of ten raised to the three. This is one thousand, one followed by three zeros. A google is one followed by one hundred zeroes—or ten thousand trillion trillion trillion trillion trillion trillion trillion trillion zeroes. At the steady rate of two zeros per second writing a google to a google out would take maybe thirty-one and a half million years, anyway, a long time. So imagine how ridiculously large a google raised to a google to a google would be.

The ultimate lifetime of our universe is thought to be about a google of years when all the protons and the largest black holes will have decayed into long-vanished radiation. According to the now increasingly accepted multiverse theory, universes of every possible description come and go throughout the infinite space that envelopes them. The greater mind-breaker— no reason to think there's any beginning or end. So we come face to face with eternity.

Because eternity is immeasurable even in thought, is it not illogical to suppose that the largest segment of time we can imagine has historical relevance? For instance, if we could visualize a google of years raised to a google of serial google exponents, this unimaginable length of time would disappear in eternity.

My Somewhat Younger Wife

My wife says I have an old person smell,
hair growing out of my nose.
My hearing's atrocious.
My heathenish notions
will certainly land me in Hell.

Then like a kitten she'll snuggle in bed,
sleep with her head on my shoulder,
laugh at a compliment, weep at a frown,
Clear as can be, I'm a hero instead.

When she tells me I'm perfect
I know that it's true.
I reply… "All the other girls
tell me that too."

She'll say "Right.
Let me trim that impeccable nose."

Proton Decay (Ziegler Madrigal Form)

Cosmologists now estimate that it will take about ten to the one hundred years for the universe to completely decay into radiation. And since there are only about ten to the eighty protons in the universe, it apparently takes about a hundred million trillion years for every proton to decay. Our universe is a mere 14 billion years old, less than one thousandth of that length of time, so it is unlikely that even one proton has yet decayed. If we imagine a proton-decay clock that ticks off one proton decay every second, each second being one hundred million trillion years, it will take close to a trillion trillion trillion trillion trillion trillion trillion trillion years before the complete nothingness alarm goes off.

It starts to get clear
best not get stuck here
with bad karma.

Mysticism (2)

Mysticism consists of convictions
that depart from God-approved orthodoxy.
Jewish mystics, for example, have in Scholem's studies
been steeped in the scriptures, the Talmud, the Zohar,
and have also perhaps studied their neighbor's wife.

More contemporary examples would include
church-going Americans who are expert pornographers
yet sing in a choir. Self-respecting gays are amazing mystics.
Good women who put up with jerks are.
I am in awe of mystics generally.

I too may be a mystic.
I have no tattoos, am straight, married, faithful—bit of a flirt maybe.
But I keep my clothes on, my lawn mowed;
and worst of all, I dabble in conventional wisdom.

I don't share this with everybody.

Sexual Intercourse

Once when I was little,
three and a half and curious,
my dad explained
the details of sexual intercourse.
I remember saying:
Ugh!
Where do you do that?
In the bathroom?

My Problem with Infinity

My problem with infinity
is knowing I am somewhere in it,
somewhere there can be nowhere.
Here I am in my pajamas
sipping coffee at five A.M. in eternity, Ha!
an interlude that likewise has no reference point.
Like having an appointment downtown
when there is no downtown, when there is no when.
Yet I'm convinced I have to keep it
or wait until next week.
So can eternity be condensed?
Can infinity be fitted into here?
Can what we see
of what must be infinite be real?
The thought occurs to me:
our blip in these monstrosities,
our palpable realities,
quantum impossibilities
perhaps, just perhaps
are incremental bits…
Get that! Incremental bits…defining what is real,
not vice versa. But then again,
any n over any infinity is zero!
Ugh! I thank God he gave me
the capacity for confusion.

So if imagination wanders
in places it can't go,
is it not a comfort to hypothesize
that all we really know for sure
is her touch, her slow
quiet little smile?

June 24

Have you noticed
that the days are getting shorter?
That the morning dark
is just a little colder?
That summer now
is more or less approved?
The stateliness of trees
in their full glory?
And how their regal leaves
already know the story
of their turning and their fall?
Their final awesome beauty
just before their fall?
A known unknown indifference
perfection can't forestall?
A small unnoticed shudder
in the stomach?

5-7-5 Haiku

Shadowy figures
moving harmoniously.
My finest vision.

Watching my elm grow,
slowly, inexorably,
the same as old age.

She asked for a ride…
her breasts pressed against my back
almost caused a wreck.

Old and dignified,
a thought informs each action.
He honors our barn.

All I have is now,
the edge of a waterfall,
enjoying the mist.

My Father

My father was a perfect man
disguised by imperfection,
imperfections I now see that can
be part of his perfection.

We had a common understanding
that the same we'd always be,
we'd never leave each other,
I was him and he was me.

As a kid I always feared him,
I rebelled against him too,
but he treated me with kindness
no matter what I'd do.

I never saw how great he was 'til I was growing old.
He visits me and comforts me,
Amazingly he sets me free
of little imperfections of my own.

Abide with Me

Abide with me
O love that will not let me go.
Abide with me
O greatness I can never know completely,
Abide with me.
Your child, your errant child
I'll always be.
What 'er befalls
I'll have with equanimity
if knowing you're beside,
inside the very depths of me.
Abide with me
O love that will not let me go,
O Presence that surrounds me,
that comforts me,
reminds me of my dignity,
that sets me free
of trouble and perplexity.
Abide with me,
whisper you'll abide with me
forever. Amen.

More 5-7-5 Haiku

May I not perform;
may I be an observer,
though interested.

Chemo companions
lead through the valley of death,
the greenest valley.

I'm retired now,
I sometimes watch my neighbor
heading off to work.

My horse has thrown me.
Heart pounding I get back on,
to be thrown again…?

Intestinal gas,
pungent, it means I'm alive.
Morning poetry.

A still cool Fall day,
The grass is cut and watered,
dinner is cooking.

Echo Cardiogram

Pathetic, quivering, struggling heart;
is this what keeps me going?
Grand surety of arrogance,
redoubtable, all-knowing!
Lo! Secret mortifying sight!
Is this the force, intrepid might,
that scales the universe at night,
that walks the cosmos,
makes it right?
that keeps my life blood flowing?
It seems a weary animal
treading out the corn
with nothing to sustain it,
unrelieved and uninformed.
I suppose this little muscle knows
it soon will be just fine
when it trades those jagged tracings
for a more composed flat line.

When the pretty cardiologist
said that she was through,
she put her finger on a spot,
she winked, she said she knew,
"When this little node is nipped,"
she said,
"you'll be as good as new."
Whoa! Watch out world!

More 5-7-5 Haiku

Safe I can live here,
less safe can go out from here.
Dangerous freedom.

I stand corrected.
My wife is smarter than I:
My undeserved luck.

Addressing my friend
creates a small disturbance.
Why would I do that?

When you approach me,
offer a hug and a kiss,
I become myself.

Big motorcycle...
astride amazing power
like a younger man.

That math-major girl...
differential equations
unbuttoned her blouse.

Driving Down the Highway

Once driving down the highway
it occurred to me—overwhelmed me like the
quiet voice of God,
a whispered certainty—
that the unanticipated moment
is precisely what is called—yes, who would guess it—
that each unnoticed moment
is what is called eternity.
I had to stop the car.
This meant the dead will live forever,
that all that is
or ever was will always be,
it meant this moment is forever,
indemnifying me...
I doubt these furious speeding cars
could see:
this infinitely small,
unpresupposing moment
is quite the same
as vast eternity.
This certainty, of course,
lasted but a moment,
and I drove on.

My Secret Tree

There comes a time,
I know it's right,
to shed illusions
that I might
proceed as always,
faltering,
to find again
the alter of myself.
Once more I'm like
the secret child
up in his secret tree
examining the bark.

Norm's New Wife

(a final chapter)

Norm's new wife
is supremely happy to be his wife.
He is the man for whom she was always looking.
She prepares healthy food
and hovers about him smiling,
like a plane about to land.
Norm stays in shape by swimming laps,
calling some old friend,
tightening up the loosened strings
of his father's violin.
They hold hands,
light candles in an empty church,
kneel and pray together.
Norm says he can hardly remember
his life in the cabin, only sometimes,
watching wild animals from his porch.
Such a compliment
that he thinks of me
and our reading sessions on PTSD.
How a man can have gone through
such danger on a flight deck,
such wretchedness at home…
How he kept smiling that
knowing smile
and have finally come to this!

Beside the Road

I have slept beside the road
like Jacob,
my head upon a stone,
and when awakening,
knowing I am home
and comforted.

How Is It

How is it
I can be so penitent
and yet not require further punishment
when I've shown myself to be
a foolish fellow?
Is it because of the time
my immortal father,
a man of the stature
of Zeus,
at the conclusion
of a financially catastrophic affair
felt so bad on the way home
that he had to stop
and buy a new Lincoln Continental?
Amazingly,
sometimes when I've been stupid
God doesn't punish me
but considers it a libation.

A Drinking Dream

A drinking dream, maybe the
worst ever.
Off and on I was considering
whether I might have a drink
or not.
I remember being persuaded,
the logic was so overwhelming
that I wondered what it was
that had kept me from seeing the light
for so long.
At the same time I was
fondling a quart of my favorite rye whiskey.
I can't remember the counterargument.

If I Had Asked

"If I had asked, would you have walked me to my car?"
Incredulous to have been asked, if only in theory,
if I would have walked her to her car.

So in half sleep
I see the buried suffering in her eyes,
a yet piquant smile.
To be invited by those eyes
to walk her to her car:
how can I breathe?
If I were to peek over
an imaginary line
(a poet has imaginary license),
I would see us walking to her car,
parked between car lines
in a parking lot
somewhere in the nearby Andromeda galaxy.
Before I bade her goodbye
I would have asked
if I might touch my finger
softly to one closed, smiling eye
in that parking lot
somewhere in the nearby Andromeda galaxy.

Watterson

Our fifth-grade teacher Mrs. Yost,
having read a book about names,
lead us one day to speculate
about the origin of our names.
I guessed that mine, Watterson,
must have been Walterson or
Waltharson, probably a legendary
Norseman,

Now, several decades later I entertain
a more likely and strangely a more satisfying origin.
From well before Roman times
the most common form of peasant construction
throughout the British Isles
was "daub and wattle":
the weaving of brushwood, "wattle",
in and out between wrist-size stakes
driven vertically into the ground.

Mud was then "daubed" into the wattle
and packed smooth. Once dry
and protected from rain it made a
reasonably durable wall.

The chief artisan in this business
would have been the "wattler"
and his boy the "wattler's son"—over time slurred into "Watterson",
Not glorious but plausible.

Freud's Lucid Comment

In a certain scene in *The Brothers Karamazov*, Dostoevsky reveals himself as nowhere else—and as nowhere else reveals the actual theme of his masterwork. I reproduce here in advance of my poem Freud's lucid comment (cf. Strachey, XXI,189f.):

"In the course of his talk with Dmitri, Father Zossima recognizes that Dmitri is prepared to commit parricide, and he bows down at his feet. It is impossible that this can be meant as an expression of admiration; it must mean that the holy man is rejecting the temptation to despise or detest the murderer and for that reason humbles himself before him. Dostoevsky's sympathy for the criminal is in fact boundless; it goes far beyond the pity which the unhappy wretch has a right to, and reminds us of the 'holy awe' with which epileptics and lunatics were regarded in the past. A criminal is to him almost a Redeemer, who has taken on himself the guilt which must else have been borne by others. There is no longer any need for one to murder, since *he* has already murdered; and one must be grateful to him, for, except for him, one would have been obliged oneself to murder. That is not kindly pity alone, it is identification on the basis of similar murderous impulses…"

My poem also tries to explain this mysterious scene. I would call it the holiness of criminals.

The Holiness of Criminals

"How can this
earth-defiling creature
be allowed to live?
Why is such a man alive?"
Our Mitya in a livid rage had said
fulminating hatred of his father,
spoken as a sacred truth,
and showed himself
a parricide.

At this, the saintly Zossima
approached him,
kneeled, and
reverently bowed low,
his brow against the ground,
unselfconsciously to show
we knew not what.
Why should such a holy man
show reverence
to one criminal as he?
Was he o'rpowered
by his Redeemer,
one who'd stayed
to set him free
of guilty passion?
In ancient Russia as we see,
lunatics and criminals
could inspire a bended knee.

Fireflies

Particle physicists now assert that
ultimate reality is an unimaginably large domain
of perfect vacuum at zero degrees Kelvin,
a condition not quite achieved in interstellar space.

The infinite, cold, absolute Nothingness
in which universes are insignificant blemishes
will contain no radiation, nothing whatever.

Yet absolute Nothingness is evidently unstable,
the source of everything,
giving rise spontaneously to "virtual particles",
most of which disappear, but some of which combine
to create hadrons, the building blocks of matter.

Given the eternity and infinity of space, universes
and clusters of universes will be inevitable throughout
like dust particles at thirty thousand feet.

And since one can now look forward to proton decay
and the evaporation of black holes, it becomes impossible
not to imagine this grand array of separate universes

as something like fireflies, winking on and off,
glowing for a moment in a summer night,
a night that has always been and will never end
here and there in an infinite back yard.

To a Girl Philosopher
Invited to the "Edge"

What we can see of the greater universe
of which we are a part
is now thought to be that of a volleyball to the
to the volume of the earth.
So one may conclude that even at inflation speed,
a speed so far undetermined—perhaps Planck time
to cross the whole thing—
still a bit of time will have elapsed
before our local cluster of universes has been crossed.
This assumes of course that universes occur in clusters everywhere
throughout an unbounded void.
So one must think that if there is no "edge" to this unending
assemblage of clusters of universes
(which must occur like unending clouds of dust particles), there must be large
gaps where nothing occurs.
Given the finitude of inflation speed and the probability that even
our local cloud of clusters can never be crossed,
we might comfort ourselves by pretending we had reached
the edge of everything. But of course we had not.
Rationality attests there can be no "edge," only distant locales
unreachable at many times inflation speed.
So if you consented home to leave

and fly with me
far, far faster than inflation speed,
you might guess
what's up my sleeve
looking for the "edge".

A Philosophy of Certainty

Preaching the certainty
of any matter,
repeatedly insisting,
(preaching),
raises the possibility
that if "certainty"
were really what it claims to be,
a steady man would find no need
to preach it.
This comforts me,
an old preachee,
though I dare not
claim much certainty
about the matter.

Cosmodirdge

In cosmodirge I'm oft inured
to the stunned companion silence
that often visits me,
a leveler that's often cured
what often troubles me.
I see for certain that I am
a grain upon this tiny earth,
this tiny turning galaxy,
these hundred billion tiny stars
lost nowhere here, some tiny, far,
just what the naked eye can see
from this tiny random speck
somewhere in this tiny unplanned vastness,
hardly here and hardly yet,
the nothingness of nothing;
in this what, this nothingness
I cannot grasp or even guess
a larger, real infinity that
unlike the Planck-length life of me
keeps going on forever.

A Transcendental Squirrel

Following a station wagon
full of happy kids
I saw a squirrel
dart beneath their car
and make it out.

But he had acquired
an awkward wobble.
He seemed not yet to know
he'd been 'nipped'
and still was heading
fast as he could go
for the safety
of his big cottonwood
beside the road.

I looked back
but for the bushes couldn't see,
but knew
he'd only make it
to the grass beneath the tree
he'd never climb.

How like that transcendental squirrel I've been
these fifty years!
emerging undeterred
between the tires,
still heading for a tree I'll never climb
with just this awkward wobble
I've acquired.

Two Ideas of God

I've taken some of the following from Wolfson, H.A., 1957, *Crescas' Critique of Aristotle*, Cambridge, Harvard University Press, pp. 123-124. (Rabbi Hasdai Crescas was born in Barcelona in 1340 and died in Saragossa in 1410. Bruno Bauer, famously obsessed with infinity, was influenced by Crescas' writings two centuries later.)

There is a suggestion in Crescas which logically could lead one to Spinoza's position of attributing extension to God. It occurs in his discussion of space. After defining space as incorporeal extension and assuming the existence of such an infinite incorporeal extension within which the world is situated, he quotes in support of his view the old rabbinic dictum that God is the place of the world... In its original sense, as used by the rabbis, it is only a pious assertion of the omnipresence of God. There is in it, however, the germ of another and radically different idea. Interpreted freely, it could be taken by one who, like Crescas, believed in the existence of an infinite space, to signify the identity of God with that infinite space or rather with the wholeness of the universe, and it would be only necessary to introduce into it the element of thought to arrive at Spinoza's novel conception of God.

Crescas, however, stops short of drawing this new conclusion from the old dictum. Indeed he starts out quite promisingly by saying that God as the place of the universe implies that He is the essence and form of the universe, which really means that God is inseparable from the universe, but without evidently realizing the significance of his own words he concludes by restoring to the dictum its original and historical sense as an assertion of the omnipresence of God within a universe from which He is separated and which He transcends.

God to him continues to play the traditional part of a transcendent being unlike anything within the universe, contrasted with it as spirit with body, as the simple with the manifold, as the actual with the potential; as the necessary with the possible. Like all other philosophers who started with such premises

Crescas found himself compelled, in order to bridge the gulf between God and the universe, to endow this transcendent God with a will and power and all the other attributes of personality, and by doing so he got himself involved in all the traditional problems of theology which form the subjects of discussion of the remaining parts of his work.

I have for many years been fascinated by the idea/image of the infinite, eternal, presumably perfect vacuum that must enclose and be the ultimate source of our universe and perhaps an unobservable multiplicity of universes. Certain philosophers (e.g., Crescas, Bauer, Spinoza) have noticed the similarity of a presumably creative, perfect, infinite and eternal space to the traditional attributes of God, attributes, at least, that do not mimic personality. Sufi and Jewish mystics centuries ago speculated that God was perfect Nothingness. For a number of years now, particle physicists have speculated that subatomic particles can form spontaneously in such a vacuum. The very ungraspability of what must be truly infinite and eternal recommends it as divine, or more than divine. Thus...

Assuming that God Is the Space in Which All Things Are Contained – Crescas' Momentary Vision

(My Interpretation)

Then God is an absolute vacuum at zero degrees Kelvin, the utter nothingness of certain Jewish and Sufi mystics, the unique identifiable *constant* of cosmology.

Being infinite, God has no center, no shape, no dimensions, no up nor down, no radiation of any kind, no gravity whatsoever. But God, the one eternal existent, evidently is, as certain particle physicists say, "unstable", and gives rise to all that is, has been or will be, the matrix of eternity.

Thus being eternal and infinite, God perdurably creates an infinite "number" of universes, a process without beginning or end. This infinite, eternal God has no human characteristics: no feelings, no intellect, no knowledge, no forgiveness, no mercy, no love. But it must be the source of everything.

From Joseph Breuer's theoretical contribution to the Breuer-Freud Studies on Hysteria, volume two of the Standard Works of Freud, ed. Strachey, pp. 209f....

"The strength of the excitation caused by the blocking of a line of associations is in direct ratio to the interest which we take in them—that is, to the degree to which they set our will in motion. Since, however, the search for a solution of the problem, or whatever it may be, always involves a large amount of work, though it may be to no purpose, even a powerful excitation finds employment and does not press for discharge, and consequently never becomes pathogenic.

It does, however, become pathogenic if the course of associations is inhibited owing to ideas of equal importance being irreconcilable—if, for instance, fresh thoughts come into conflict with old-established ideational complexes. Such are the torments of religious doubt to which many people succumb and many more succumbed in the past. Even in such cases, however, the excitation and the accompanying psychical pain (the feeling of unpleasure) only reach any considerable height if some volitional interest of the subject's comes into play—if, for instance, a doubter feels himself threatened in the matter of his happiness or his salvation. Such a factor is always present, however, when the conflict is one between firmly-rooted complexes of moral ideas in which one has been brought up and the recollection of actions or merely thoughts of one's own which are irreconcilable with them; when, in other words, one feels the pangs of conscience. It is a matter of everyday experience that a conflict like this between irreconcilable ideas has a pathogenic effect."

To a Dignified Lady

Is it possibly not wise
to walk you to your car?
to boldly ask
to touch your soft eye lids,
this downy amber porcelain?

…to mention walking to a star,
the bright one say
between those winter branches?

…convince you it's a special star,
a galaxy that's not too far to walk to…a star we've just invented?

or share our memories in the night,
and feel the breeze?
or see by the seraphic light
inviting genies rising from a bottle?

or feel delights that maybe cannot be?
O God! O God!

If you should let me touch your eyes
I know I'd trembling ask
if wisdom's always
always wise?

I know I'd have to ask,
I needn't know.

Compunction

Suspecting that I've come too far
to find my way back home,
I'd hope there'll be some lucky star
to guide me, tell me not to roam
on solitary travels any more.

Rather to read some vital tome,
content like Badger 'neath his tree,
to know it's best to be alone,
ensconced in grave philosophy,
like Arthur Schopenhauer.

I'll get used to being old,
to limit working to an hour,
to nap, refrain from being bold;
content with turning pages 'til I'm sleepy.

An Image of My Wife

Of Franz Liszt's Hungarian Rhapsodies, the sixth,
she said, her favorite place of all,
the long-awaited marching part,
that swells and gladdens every heart.
was what was next on my CD.
I turned it up.
The lights turned off, the car was dark,
we were late and I'd just parked
so I only saw it indistinctly—her small hands were lifted up
as if floating unconsciously,
lilting to that marching heart-like beat.

Had I ever seen this innocence,
her nothing-hidden child-like face,
for just the smallest moment
caught up in unrelenting grace?
Responding to that rhapsody, wrapped in private happiness,
something I know I'd never seen
even in a dream of her
quite like that before?

This lasted just a moment, as I said,
but this now-embedded hologram
of her living, lifting, little hands
to this favorite passage keeping time,
has become a holy talisman

that fills my heart with pain
and a love that makes me sad
to see I'm such a selfish
unobservant man.

Supernatural Wisdom

My wondrous wife is always happy
with the poor things I can give her.
She's a wellspring of affection,
of church-going modesty.
She often says, "I love you,
I'm so glad that you love me."
Her smile is bright, the purest light
this errant man could ever see.
Each afternoon she'll lay her head—she'll ask me this to do—
so lightly on my chest and sleep—the sweetest thing—
an hour or so or sometimes two
and often let me longer nap,
and wake me gently
with a snack and
with my favorite cup of tea
Can you imagine what a firestorm
my loving wife would be
should she catch me with some
other friendly woman?
Whoa! Forget that!

The Illusion

The illusion
that everything will stay
the same
is not just a constant companion
and comfort,
but a whispering terror of
unending change.
The merciless tide ineluctance
informs me that earthquakes
await at the door.
I'm ready, I'm ready,
I'm ready I cry.
I'm a veteran of trouble,
so what's a bit more?
Change after change
have I left in my lee.
Will there be more surprises?
Indubitably.

At a Gas Stop East of Reno

At a gas stop east of Reno
I encountered my ideal
I'd swear that man was ninety-two.
Though somewhat younger I could feel
the sovereign loneliness
I'd chanced to run into.

He'd filled his scooter up with fuel
and stayed to take a nap
on a piece of rolled out plastic
where there was a bit of grass
next to the filling station.
He had a Cushman scooter, Model 52
—kind I'd wanted as a kid
—'course I'd wanted one much newer,
one that still was shiny red.

A milk carton full of camping gear
was bolted on the back.
You could see he was a gentleman,
the thoughtful way he moved,
checking out and loading up
his hobo Cadillac.

Was he too old for Korea?
Did he maybe know my dad?
…On that hill on Iwo Jima
did he help to raise the flag?

I boldly asked him
"Where ya goin'?"
"Just down the road," he said.
"Next rest stop I'll be campin' out,
my tent's here in the load.

You'd be amazed," he volunteered,
"how far these things can go.
Might even ride her out of state."
(Was "out of state" a metaphor
I wondered?)

He climbed up on the pedal
using all his weight:
"put put put put" it started up.
Like him it sounded hopeful
if a little low on oil.

He waved goodbye—I see him still—
astride that Cushman scooter
sitting ramrod straight,
and heading
for his next adventure.

Though I was barely sixty then
I felt a bath of glory when
this feather, this now sainted man
forever blew away.

Here

Here in my study
book-lined walls protect me,
friendly conspiring pages.
In an instant I participate
in a long-lost reverie,
lifting from the page
a thought I prize,
a conclusion I've
waited for.
In quiet,
safety
and peace
I sink in my chair
remembering Isaiah,
anticipating the scent,
the dusty scent I've waited for.
Like Rat I know the scent,
the scent of nearing my home.

Love at Seventy Once Again

Only a glimpse of my wife
depressed in the car beside me.

The 6th Hungarian Rhapsody was on,
that slow emphatic part
—her favorite—was about to start.
She began conducting the air,
all sadness there suspended,

her face sublime, carried away,
her lifted hand was keeping time—a moment of happiness.

That glimpse is now forever mine.
The rhapsody is now divine.
I didn't know I loved her that much.

Aphorisms, New Ideals as I Age

When I see the shadow
of the man I thought was me,
let me ask at every sunrise…
if like the aging Socrates
I dance to raise the sun.
Yes.
I know there is a chance
my aging shadow will be cast
across the universe, even if not
catching up and dancing
with my hero.

A Fly

I was sitting beside Denise waiting for the meeting to start.
A fly was bothering me.
I waited until it landed beside me,
and clapped my hands and got it,
but it was only wounded
and soon got up and started walking around looking normal,
but it couldn't fly.
Was that just PTSD? I'd clapped him pretty hard.
I thumped it across the table trying to finish it off,
but the fly was still okay and walked around just the same.
I tried thumping it again but missed.
Now I considered it my pet fly.
So then it walked over right in front of me
showing me his spirit and daring me to kill him.
I couldn't.
I knew he was reproaching me,
and I remained reproached all evening.
Reproached by a fly!

A Bell Pepper

In 1943 I became five going on six.
Friday afternoons I would get my nickel allowance.
What was memorable about this
was that two kids I knew would be in the
White Swan Grocery Store at the same time
with their nickels. Must have been
some sort of tradition our mothers adhered to.
There was always the same perplexity
about what to get.
Wendel would ponder slowly
over the candy bars, never satisfied with his choice.
I might get something like a fudgesickle.
Robert, who seldom said anything
was a mystery:
he would get a big green bell pepper
and crunch it on the way out of the store.
Robert was original with that bell pepper.
He became a philosopher.
He was already a peeping tom.

I Pledge Allegiance

"I pledge allegiance to the flag…"
Miss Miller would stop:
"Johnny, firmly like this!"
That would make her nipples show.
But I was already patriotic.

All That Is

Supposing all that is
is enclosed in an infinite nothingness,
and taking this as reality…
my first conclusion would be that
because anything however large
divided by infinity equals zero,
everything we say exists does not
exist in the large view.
This is my first conclusion,
troublesome of course,
because the physical reality we know
seems certain.
The latter homespun view votes down
the first conclusion.
An understanding certified by common
experience is that what we perceive is real.
In that lucky case what is set over infinity
or what appears to be infinity
might not reduce to zero.
The denominator must be less than infinity,
silly as that sounds.
So speculation always being second choice
in such matters, the here and now
muscles its way in and becomes authoritative.
The argument will start all over again
and become serious if some future monster telescope
can detect nothing out there.
Could some cosmic thought police be listening?

Does a Blade of Grass...?

have awareness of itself?
Awareness of sunlight,
of the starry sky above?
A better grasp of all that is,
the happiness of knowing
a silent music everywhere,
so that each blade of grass
can join in fellowship—
a myriad grassy choir
in upward strophic harmony,
unknown grassy voices
that make a grassy symphony,
spontaneous conspiracy,
or reckless
silent
unplanned
grassy jamming
in the backyard in the dark?

No

No, there's nothing wrong,
it's just I'm suddenly contrite,
it's just old age,
it's just the fading light

No, there's nothing wrong
I like to say,
it's just my friends have passed away,
their fading light is gone.

No, life is good I have to say,
just like is written on my cap.

The Nihilist

For the cosmic nihilist
there is no beginning
and can be no end.
And worst of all no nothing.
He is pleased to think of nothing
(nothing is his favorite).
But he's afraid there might not be
any nothing after all,
or if there is, not enough.
If there is truly nothing
he prefers nothing more than that.
The world is full of idiots
who believe in something.
Not him.
Against all odds he believes
in nothing at all.
And even nothing is a bit much.

A Certain Manly Quality

There is a certain
manly quality
I'm not sure I've ever had...
a quiet smiling confidence
my uncle Glenn called bluffing.
But if 'bluffing', it was godly.
What made it godly
was that mixture of confidence
and kindness that says:
"I know that you know too,
you rascal."
Such a man is beyond being lovable,
He needn't claim love,
he is already everything.

The End?

Trapped in old age,
Avoiding the exit.